URBAN OBSESSIONS
URBAN FEARS

URBAN OBSESSIONS
URBAN FEARS:

THE POSTCOLONIAL KENYAN
NOVEL

J. Roger Kurtz

Africa World Press, Inc.

P.O. Box 1892
Trenton, NJ 08607

P.O. Box 48
Asmara, ERITREA

Africa World Press, Inc.

P.O. Box 1892
Trenton, NJ 08607

P.O. Box 48
Asmara, ERITREA

Copyright © 1998 J. Roger Kurtz

First Printing 1998

Book design: Wanjiku Ngugi
Cover design: Jonathan Gullery

Library of Congress Cataloging-in-Publication Data

Kurtz, John Roger.
    Urban obsessions, urban fears : the postcolonial Kenyan novel / by J. Roger Kurtz.
      p.   cm.
    Includes bibliogrpahical references and index.
    ISBN 0-86543-656-8. -- ISBN 0-86543-657-6 (pbk.)
    1. Kenyan fiction (English)--History and criticism. 2. Literature and society--Kenya--History--20th century. 3. Rural-urban migration in literature. 4. City and town life in literature. 5. Cities and towns in literature. 6. Decolonization in literature. I. Title.
    PR9381.4.K87 1998
    823--dc21   98-34805
                                       CIP

Published in England by:

James Currey Ltd.
73 Botley Road
Oxford, OX2 OBS

CONTENTS

Preface

When I tell people in Nairobi that I am interested in the country's literature, the spontaneous response—from Kenyans and non-Kenyans alike—is typically one of surprise: "Oh, *is* there any?" they might ask; or just as often, "Well, you won't find much."

My hope is that this study, the first full-length examination of the anglophone Kenyan novel, can help eradicate some of the misconceptions about the nation's literature. Readers, I hope, will come to appreciate the scope, the preoccupations, and also the problems of the contemporary novel in Kenya. Clearly, there *is* a significant body of Kenyan novels that has developed over the past thirty years. At the end of this volume is, for the first time in one place, a comprehensive and annotated list of anglophone Kenyan novels; they number something over 200 titles.

Beyond noting the volume of Kenya's writing, however, this study also seeks to explore the connections of literature with the vital problems that have come to be called Third World development issues. To an extent not seen in many others areas of the world, African literatures are closely connected with the broader social contexts in which they are produced. In my reading of Kenya's novels, I have been impressed by how important the city is, as a setting that is also a symbol for so many of the dynamics of postcolonial society.

This project saw its beginnings in the University of Iowa's comparative literature program, where my interests, somewhat unorthodox by many standards, were supported and encouraged. A Fulbright-Hays research scholarship allowed me to do the bulk of the research; the Office of the President of the Republic of Kenya kindly granted research clearance for the study.

In Kenya, I am especially indebted to Francis Imbuga and others at Kenyatta University's department of language and literature: Nana Tagoe, Mrs. Olembo, Austin Bukenya and others have made me welcome. I am also grateful to the many Kenyan writers and publishers—too many to thank individually—who have been so willing to discuss their experiences with me. Others in Nairobi provided personal and professional encouragement at key stages of the project: Calestous Juma at the African Center for Technology Studies (ACTS), Kabiru Kinyanjui, Harold and Annetta Miller, others in the Mennonite Central Committee offices, Bironyi Sadiki and other friends at Eastleigh.

Staff at various Nairobi libraries have been of immense assistance. I am particularly grateful to Ruth Thomas at the Library of Congress field offices in Nairobi. Thanks also go to the librarians at the University of Nairobi, Kenyatta University, Hekima College, the Macmillan Library and the National Archives. Staff at the Institute for Development Studies helped me find elusive back issues of IDS papers, and the Ministry of Information assisted me in wading through their photo files, featuring fascinating images of early Nairobi.

Finally, I am grateful to my family—parents Maynard and Hilda, and brothers Robert and Eric—who have demonstrated for me how to read and live in both Third and First Worlds with integrity and joy.

The City, the Novel, and Postcolonial Kenya

To date, there has been no comprehensive, scholarly examination of the Kenyan novel. Book-length studies on the subject have tended toward one of two approaches, either addressing a single author or theme—Ngugi wa Thiong'o or the
Mau Mau experience, for example—or discussing a few sa-
lient Kenyan texts as part of a broader, continentwide or regional study of African writing. Both approaches have generated an important and growing body of critical analysis over
the last twenty years; each has contributed considerably to
our understanding and appreciation of Kenyan literature. The
present study, however, takes something of a middle ground
between these two approaches: Its object is the anglophone
Kenyan novel as a whole, with special attention to the representation of the city in those texts.

There are a number of difficulties with these parameters—
at once linguistic (anglophone), geopolitical (Kenyan) and
formal (the novel)—since there are inevitably texts that test
each of them. Who, for example, qualifies as a Kenyan author? Throughout the 1960s and early 1970s, many writers
thought of themselves and each other in terms of a strongly

regional literary identity; they were East African writers, in addition to being from Kenya, Tanzania, or Uganda. Following the break-up of the East African Community, however, separate national identities became much more significant, although not always self-evident.

National categories are not always the most useful for defining postcolonial forms of cultural expression. For one thing, they gloss over regional dynamics. Kenya's Ngugi, for example, like many of his contemporaries, spent formative years at Makerere College in Uganda. When Taban lo Liyong taught at the University of Nairobi, he was identified as a Ugandan, although he has since insisted on his Sudanese origins. National categories also fail to allow for more fundamental cultural commonalities: because of her Luo heritage, Kenya's Grace Ogot has far more in common culturally with Uganda's Okot p'Bitek, an Acoli, than with many of her Kenyan compatriots.

An additional dilemma surfaces in deciding whom to include from the category known as "expatriate writers" in Kenya. My criteria exclude such writers as Elspeth Huxley, Isak Dinesen and others because, even though the writers themselves were arguably *from* Kenya, their writing targeted an expatriate, non-African audience and addressed specifically expatriate concerns. Theirs is literature of Kenya's settler community. Huxley and Dinesen, their writing shows, saw themselves primarily as members of a European diaspora in the Kenya colony and only secondarily as Kenyans. By these same criteria, writers like Marjorie Oludhe Macgoye and Yusuf Dawood, although not African by birth, may be considered Kenyan writers.

Further difficulty arises in determining what exactly qualifies as a novel, particularly an anglophone novel. Experimental writers like David Maillu and Muthoni Likimani sometimes blur the distinctions between poetry and prose, employing blank verse in the tradition of Okot p'Bitek's songs, or (as in the case of David Maillu's unique novella, *Without Kiinua*

Mgongo) by playing havoc with the anglophone part of the definition by writing in a macaronic mixture of languages that we might call "Swahinglish." Ngugi wa Thiong'o is technically no longer an anglophone writer, following his widely publicized decision to compose only in Kikuyu or in Swahili, although he began his literary career as one. His more recent works have been made available in English translation immediately after their release in Kikuyu. To top it all off, the recent boom in popular literature in Kenya challenges the standard distinction between literature (in its more formal sense) and juvenile or young adult fiction.

The above-mentioned considerations are more than simple inconveniences for the student of African literatures. They are inherent in the dynamics of contemporary Kenyan writing and demonstrate a point that will become evident in the chapters that follow. In postindependence Kenya, both the novel as a form of creative expression and the notion of the nation-state as a primary community have been in a state of constant flux and crisis. The former, with some significant exceptions, has for various reasons become stuck in an imitative rather than an innovative mode, while the latter is being increasingly challenged by allegiances to linguistic, religious, or class affiliations. Both novel and nation defy simple classification and categorization.

Despite the difficulties, it is nevertheless possible to speak of an entity called the anglophone Kenyan novel that has developed over the past thirty-five years, beginning with Ngugi wa Thiong'o's *Weep Not, Child* (1964) and currently comprising approximately 200 titles (which are listed in Part Three). Because Kenya attained political independence in 1963, this body of texts corresponds closely to the postindependence era; the Kenyan novel is by definition "postcolonial," in the most literal sense of the term. While the novel in Kenya demonstrates a great deal of variety, one of its most remarkable features, which allows us to understand it in general terms, is its pronounced emphasis on the city.

Much has been made, and rightly so, of the historical connections between the city and the novel. Observers as diverse as Ian Watt and Raymond Williams have demonstrated how the realist novel in nineteenth-century Britain was a response to the exigencies of an expanding urban population in an increasingly industrialized system of social and economic production. In the late twentieth century, critical attention to postmodern urban geographies and their relation to various forms of cultural production, including the novel, has contributed to literary and cultural studies in innovative and fundamental ways. What has not been examined in any depth, however, is the city-novel connection in the postcolonial African setting. Despite the burgeoning fascination with postcolonial literatures, and despite the decidedly geographical imagery of many of the models of postcolonial narrative, most of the debate surrounding these texts has focused on factors of race, language, and gender in the construction of colonial and postcolonial subjectivity rather than on geographical issues of spatiality. This study reasserts that connection by exploring postcolonial narrative practice and its relation to postcolonial urban geography in the Kenyan setting. It is my contention that the city and the novel are inextricably linked in postcolonial Kenya; to understand one, we would do well to understand the other.

Since its beginnings a century ago as an unpretentious railway depot on the line to Uganda, Nairobi has grown into the largest and most important urban center in the East African region. In the process, it has progressed through a series of growing pains and crises as its role has shifted from a depot to an administrative site to a "White man's city" at the center of a settler colony, and finally to a postcolonial capital connecting East Africa with the global economy. Its story resembles those of many other postcolonial capitals, but what is most fascinating in all these transitions is the image of Nairobi in the popular imagination. If the colonial ideal was of a paradisal "green city in the sun" (which remains Nairobi's motto to this day), the postcolonial image is somewhat more complex.

The image of Nairobi as paradise is by no means dead, but Kenyan writers have been complicating the picture considerably in the thirty years since independence: Meja Mwangi's well-known urban trilogy—*Kill Me Quick*, *Going Down River Road*, and *The Cockroach Dance*—has become the paradigm for the exposure of Nairobi's urban underbelly; popular texts such as those from Charles Mangua and David Maillu alternately celebrate the opportunities amid the bright lights of the city or excoriate its corrupt, parasitical nature; writers like Marjorie Oludhe Macgoye, meanwhile, record the ways that ordinary Nairobians manage to find hope and home in this often hostile urban environment. It is through investigating the various layers of images present in Kenyan writing that we can begin to understand the nature of such a place as postcolonial Nairobi.

More than images must be examined of course, since space—especially urban space—is, above all, a social product. The questions raised in this type of investigation are inveterately linked to broader issues pertaining to what is generally termed Third World development. One can suggest that the most useful way to negotiate the connections between the postcolonial city and the postcolonial novel is to see both as complex, hybrid creations. Each was born of the interaction of indigenous social forms and institutions with imported (in most cases, European) social forms and institutions, and each has taken shape within the opportunities and constraints they offer. This interaction is a complicated and overdetermined process, yielding multifaceted and often contradictory results both in the urban landscape and in the urban novel.

In examining the development of the Kenyan novel, it becomes clear that a defining characteristic of the genre is its fascination with urbanization. The city, especially Nairobi, is present in almost all Kenyan novels, and is a dominant feature in most of them. The overarching theme of this study, which provides the descriptive half of its title, is that the city is where Kenyan novelists regularly project both the obsessions and the fears of their society. In examining the nature and content of these projections, we can also learn much about the dynamics of an increasingly urbanized Kenyan society and the particular forms of cultural expression—especially novels—that it has engendered.

Such a study necessarily invokes a dual focus. First, it requires a discussion of Kenya's urban geography, with particular attention to Nairobi. What are the challenges, problems, and opportunities of urbanization specific to contemporary Nairobi? What are the unique features of the postcolonial East African city in the late twentieth century? The second focus is, therefore, an investigation of the development and role of the Kenyan novel in relation to and in the context of the city. The question, then, becomes: How have Kenyan writers represented and reproduced the dynamics of urbanization that are unique to contemporary Nairobi?

There are several important preliminary points to be made about the postcolonial novel's relation to the postcolonial city. Most obvious is that urbanization is one of the most significant social phenomena in Kenya today. Although East Africa is, by global standards, a relatively underurbanized region, the rate of urban growth in Kenya is extremely high. Since its founding, Nairobi has been in a constant state of rapid growth, and more recently the other major urban centers (Mombasa, Kisumu, Nakuru, Thika and Eldoret) have also grown dramatically. In Kenya, where the population growth rate was, until recently, regularly cited as being among the highest in the world, the urban growth rate is double that of the nation as a whole. Such rapid urbanization is straining an already stressed infrastructure and social service system; like many Third World cities, Nairobi is in a state of crisis. Urban centers throughout the country are growing rapidly, but Nairobi remains the overwhelmingly dominant city in the region and will therefore absorb most of our attention.

Sheer numbers aside, the city is most important because of its role as the primary locus for the basic conflicts and contradictions in contemporary African society. An accepted truth in urban studies is that city and hinterland are inveterately linked, and that we cannot understand one without analyzing its connections to the other. If anything, this is even more the case in a place like Kenya, since Nairobi and other urban centers were historically established for the sole purpose of connecting the East African interior to the world economy. In fact, there are three important spaces in the geography of postcolonial Africa: rural hinterlands, cities, and, as geographers sometimes call them, the metropoles—the economic centers of Europe, America or Asia. The city is where the hinterlands meet the metropoles, and the resulting conflicts have been described in various ways: as the meeting of South and North, of literate and oral cultures, or of tradition and modernity. The most basic dynamic, however, is economic, as the postcolonial city is the primary intersection point for global (usually European) capitalism and noncapitalist African social formations.

It is precisely these conflicts and contradictions that have obsessed most Kenyan—indeed, most African—writers, whether or not they set their texts in the city. The city is the site where those conflicts are most evident, so that even in those rare cases where the city is totally absent from a text, it becomes significant by that absence. It is thus no surprise that Nairobi plays a key role in the most compelling and original novels from Kenya.

The novel and the city are furthermore linked in Kenya today because both represent recently imported forms that reflect the tensions of that importation. The postcolonial novel and the postcolonial city are, like contemporary African society as a whole, the products of four predominant social influences: the fundamental experience of the colonial encounter, the political reality of the East-West superpower conflict and its aftermath, the economic constraints of international capital, and the underlying heritage of indigenous African traditions. These influences overlay, interweave and swirl together in fascinating and chaotic ways. City and novel are products of these realities and their interactions. City and novel—the constructed environment and the creative environment—at the same time influence and shape those interactions.

Reading Kenyan novels is important for anyone who wishes to understand and appreciate the urban geography of the country. Novels are not necessarily roadmaps, but they do provide insights into the society that produced them. They show us that a city cannot be assessed merely by the shape of its skyline or by its population. There is more to a city, they remind us, than meets the eye. Fiction, sometimes unintentionally, offers imaginative descriptions of social reality and prescriptions for the social ills they present. In surveying the history of the Kenyan novel, it becomes clear that Kenyan writers have always offered clues to understanding the postcolonial city, and that they are likely to continue doing so. Furthermore, fiction contains truths that often have no other outlet, and Kenyan writers have been able to say critical things about the city that social scientists have not—particularly in the past two decades, an era in which political and social dissent have been increasingly stifled in Kenya.

Now, at the start of the twenty-first century, African society finds itself at a unique historical conjuncture. A generation after independence, illusions about the fruits of seeking and gaining the political kingdom, to use Nkrumah's phrase, have been largely shattered. The promises of pan-Africanism and African nationalism have been largely unfulfilled. The end of the Cold War has radically changed the geopolitical realities of the continent. In many ways, Africa is more than ever becoming the forgotten continent, more peripheral than ever to the global political economy.

If there is a positive side to these developments, it is perhaps that artists and novelists, those who create and nourish the myths and stories of a community, have an unusual opportunity to create new myths and tell new stories. It is my hope that this study of the first generation of Kenyan novels will provide a useful basis for thinking about the limits and possibilities of the next.

Part One offers a chronological overview of the Kenyan novel, beginning with its broadest historical outlines (Chapter One); moving on to the "first generation" novels of the 1960s (Chapter Two); the "golden age" of the 1970s (Chapter Three); and developments in the novel during the post-Kenyatta era of the 1980s and 1990s (Chapter Four).

Part Two focuses on the relations between the postcolonial novel and the postcolonial city, examining how the various obsessions and fears about urbanization have entered the postcolonial literary imagination through Kenya's novelists. It outlines how the portrayal of the city changed through the various eras of Kenyan writing (Chapter Five) and examines the close connections between urban concerns and the dramatic explosion in popular literature (Chapter Six). The section concludes with specific and in-depth discussions of two topics: first, the work of Meja Mwangi, which may be considered paradigmatic of the various ways Kenyan writers have responded to urbanization (Chapter Seven); and second, what Kenyan novels tell us about the paradoxical nature of the city in relation to gender (Chapter Eight).

Part Three, finally, consists of an annotated bibliography of the anglophone Kenyan novel from 1964 to the present.

Part I

A Brief History
of the Kenyan Novel

Chapter 1

Literary Barrenness?
The Historical Context

The history of the novel in East Africa is a relatively short one. The region's coastal areas and their corresponding islands have produced an elaborate, centuries-old tradition of Swahili written verse in a variety of regional dialects, featuring an extensive corpus of *hadithi* (tales), love poetry, religious writing, and epic historical verse. The inland regions feature a rich tradition of oral narrative, in which there has been a greatly renewed interest of late. But the novel itself is a recent European import that came to East Africa—as elsewhere—as part of the broader cultural baggage constituting European colonial expansion in the late nineteenth and early twentieth centuries. The first novels from the region were produced by expatriate settlers and visitors, i.e., Europeans such as Isak Dinesen, Elspeth Huxley, and Robert Ruark. Novels by Kenyans themselves only appeared following independence. The story of the novel in Kenya, therefore, is a recent story, whose significance lies in how this alien form has been received and transformed in its new setting.

Clearly, this type of transplantation is unlikely to be simple or straightforward under any circumstances. The novel's development in Kenya might remind us of its history in England, where it appeared as one cultural manifestation of a changing, industrializing economy that resulted in increasing individualism, the growth of literacy, and the development of an enlarged leisure class. Not surprisingly, however, the Kenyan novel also presents some unique features.

Looking at the European literary tradition from a remove of several centuries, it is now tempting to see its development as inevitable, as if there were a logical and predictable shape to the evolution of literary forms. What we find in examining the Kenyan situation, however, is that although novelists are profoundly compelled and limited by their society, very little of what they do may be characterized as inevitable. We can only be impressed by the way that some novelists have transcended whatever expectations we might have, while others have failed to live up to them. This chapter introduces the variety of ways that Kenyan writers have responded to the challenges of working with an alien cultural form in the process of creating what is now a sizable and unique novelistic tradition and the particular conditions and challenges that these writers have faced.

Since its inception, East African writing in English has suffered from two related pathologies: an inferiority complex on the one hand, and an identity crisis on the other. Neither phenomenon, it should be noted, is in any way unusual in a new or emerging literary tradition. East Africa's sense of literary inferiority was articulated first and most forcefully by the Ugandan/Sudanese writer and critic Taban lo Liyong, who minces no words in his pessimistic assessment of East African literature in his ode, "East Africa, O East Africa / I lament thy literary barrenness." The poem originally appeared in a 1965 issue of East Africa's first independent literary and cultural journal, *Transition: (volume 19)*

> When will the Nile basin find a Dickens? Or a Conrad?
> Or a Mark Twain? Or a Joyce Cary? Is a Rudyard

> Kipling coming to Mowgli our national parks? . . .
> We need Ngugis in plural to do a la Guma job between
> a capital letter and a period. Come, come songsters,
> work our sentiments and emotions, and instincts hot
> and cool. Weave your flirting flitting yarns on natural
> objects. Pour forth your hearts' contents on a morale-
> creating-destroying fashion-wise world. (11)

Curiously enough, Taban's manifesto remains the starting point for much of the critical literary discussion in Kenya even to-day: The commonplace formula is for reviewers and critics to remind their readers of Taban's essay and then to discuss how the writer or text under discussion either proves or disproves the continuing validity of his claim that East Africa is a wilderness with respect to literary achievement. What is most noteworthy about Taban's lament is not so much the claim that East Africa constituted a literary desert, but rather the areas with which he chose to draw his comparisons. Instead of measuring the region against the European literary tradition (although he makes plenty of references to it), Taban was mainly concerned with how East Africa fared in comparison with West and Southern Africa, both of which had at the time produced a relative wealth of literary material.

Taban is no stranger to controversy, and his comments aroused objections to its reliance on a Western conception of "literature" as a measure of the similarly Western-defined notions of "progress" and "civilization." Nonetheless, even his harshest critics had to admit that Taban had a certain point. East African writing in the early 1960s was, as he claimed, constrained by "political grievances (about land, mostly) and answering back the white racist charges through pamphlets, and biographies and anthropological works," rather than being free to produce literary works on its own terms.

The paucity of East African writing in English, relative to other areas of the continent, had become rather obvious several years earlier, as the result of an important conference that was held at what was then Makerere University College in

Kampala. This first African Writers' Conference, in 1962, featured established African authors such as Chinua Achebe, John Pepper Clark, Wole Soyinka, and Kofi Awoonor from West Africa, and Ezekiel Mphahlele and William "Bloke" Modisane from South Africa. Even though Uganda served as conference host and could lay claim to holding the continent's leading institution of higher education, it could not boast of any established writers at the time. The most promising event for East Africans was James Ngugi's play, *The Black Hermit*, which premiered as part of the event. Consequently, in addition to boosting African writing in general, the conference served as a challenge to East African writers in particular. It also promoted an important debate about elitism and literature's role in "Third World" society, an issue that was to feature prominently in East African writing—not least of all in the Kenyan novel—in the ensuing decades.

Regarding the second pathology in East African writing, the crisis of identity, three developments in particular are worth noting, each of them resulting in fundamental changes in the nature of East African writing over the past three decades. First, ever since the African Writers' Conference at Makerere, there has been a growing emphasis on national identity at the expense of regional affiliations; second, there has been an improvement and a subsequent decline in the quality and the role of higher education institutions in the region; and third, there have been increasing ideological divisions over the role of the writer in society, resulting in a tension between serious or "committed" writers and popular authors.

The first development is political in its origins. At its inception, Kenyan literature was inseparable from the broader East African literary tradition. Before independence and even through the 1960s, the region's writers tended to classify themselves as East Africans first and foremost, an identification that was clearly understandable in light of the economic and cultural ties set forth initially under British rule and later by the establishment of the East African Economic Community

(EAEC). The African Writers' Conference at Makerere in 1962 and the founding of the East African Publishing House in 1966 took for granted this regional literary identity. In the years that followed, however, there was a notable shift in this regard among East Africa's writers, who today classify themselves as primarily Kenyan, Tanzanian, or Ugandan. This shift was institutionalized by the final break-up of the EAEC in 1977, although it had begun somewhat earlier. In any case, national identity has in recent years become more prominent than the pan-African or regional identities that were more evident in the immediate postindependence era.

It should be noted that the intertwined trajectories of literature and nationalism are by no means peculiar to Kenya, since they have close historical links in most parts of the world. In Kenya, however, the two are married in an especially tight, and ironic, manner. The standardization of Zanzibari Swahili through the efforts of Bishop Steere in the late 1800s and the establishment of an East African Swahili Committee in 1930 were part of an attempt to unify East Africa as a political and economic unit; central to this task was the promotion of writing in Swahili. At the same time, and somewhat contradictorily, British colonial authorities were eager to maintain "tribal" affiliations and identities as a way of preventing united opposition to British rule. "Detribalization"—the establishment of loyalties and identities broader than the tribal unit—was seen as a threat to British power, and one way to prevent it from developing was by reinforcing vernacular languages and literatures. Consequently, the East African Literature Bureau was founded in 1948 with the express purpose of publishing in indigenous languages. Writing in English by Kenyans was certainly not openly promoted. It was only with Kenyan independence that an anglophone literature was encouraged and able to develop, largely as a way of promoting national unity. It is thus an irony of Kenya's literary history that the development of a literature in English was to occur only after the end of British rule.

The second factor concerning identity is institutional. During the first generation of postindependence writing, the region's universities were the main source of creative activity. Taban lo Liyong, Ngugi wa Thiong'o, and others energized East African literature and literary debate from their university posts. Around 1970, there was a well-known discussion of the role of language, literary form and the relationship of literature to society at the University of Nairobi, which ultimately resulted in the dismantling of the English Department and replacing it with a Department of Literature at that university. In the same era, Makerere University in Uganda had established a reputation as the premier institution of higher education on the continent, while the University of Dar es Salaam in Tanzania was an intellectual hotbed for discussions of social reform.

Since then, however, the universities have lost their status as the primary site for cutting-edge social and cultural debate. Makerere was effectively dismantled under the Idi Amin regime in the early 1970s, while elsewhere a lack of resources, combined with political interference, has driven away outspoken scholars and stifled critical debate. The positive slant to this otherwise demoralizing development has been that writers have emerged from outside the university community. Meja Mwangi, having established his reputation as a writer long before going on to complete a bachelor's degree at Leeds, is an early example from Kenya. Playwright Okoiti Omtatah and novelists Thomas Akare, Moses Ndissio-Otieno, and Margaret Ogola are further examples of this trend, which seems likely to continue.

The third development involves a basic ideological shift in much East African writing. Texts from the first generation of writers, which were profoundly and almost exclusively characterized by an involvement in and a commitment to nation-building and social improvement, were suddenly confronted with a new, post-1970 body of writing that by and large lacked that commitment. The critical debate in the first generation of writers centered on what it meant to be committed writers and how artists might most effectively contribute to society through their art. More recently, however, the market has been flooded by texts that are generally and pejoratively lumped under the term "popular literature." Because they fail to address the problems of East African society seriously, these texts have been roundly condemned, but thanks to their immense popularity they continue to dominate the Kenyan market. No longer is it assumed that to be a writer is to concern oneself with issues of social justice.

These broader problems—inferiority complex and identity crisis—become more understandable when placed in historical and geographical perspective. In response to Taban's lament, there are obviously a number of important reasons why West and Southern Africa have produced more novels than Kenya. For one thing, the vehicles for these cultural forms in Africa, colonialism and its institutions, have been in place there several generations longer than in East Africa. A host of other economic, political, and social factors are at work as well, including the state of the economy in general and the publishing industry in particular. The effective dismantling of East Africa's universities, for instance, which must be understood as an attempt by the state to suppress a potentially strong source of political opposition, cut short a promising source of literary advancement as well. In short, it is crucial to appreciate the realities of East Africa's history and geography in order to understand the development of the Kenyan novel.

Despite all these challenges, the Kenyan novel has developed in remarkable and often unique ways. To date, Kenyan novelists have proven far more prolific than their counterparts from other countries in the region, again for understandable reasons: In Uganda, economic and cultural life on all levels disintegrated dramatically during the Idi Amin era; while in Tanzania, the cultural policies encouraged the development of Swahili-language writing. Consequently, one result of the break-up of the EAEC was that Kenya—and Nairobi in particular—became the publishing capital of the region, and the source of the most dynamic developments in the anglophone novel.

It is possible to divide the history of the Kenyan novel in three broad, chronological categories: (1) the "first generation" novels from the years immediately following independence; (2) a brief "golden age" in the 1970s, featuring a remarkable boom in the quantity of published novels, along with an impressive augmentation and elaboration of their thematic repertoire; and (3) the post-Kenyatta years of the 1980s and 1990s, in which innovations have continued despite a marked decrease in the overall quantity of new works.

Like any categorization, this one is necessarily arbitrary. One could discuss the Kenyan novel thematically, in which case a variety of major strands would emerge: a revisiting and evaluation of the Mau Mau experience, the conflict between traditional and modern values, criticism of the neocolonial elite, the urban thriller, the suburban romance, and so forth. Alternatively, it would be possible to discuss the works on the basis of geographical or ethnic categories, in which case the dominance of Kikuyu writing would be evident and the thematic concerns of writers from the country's various regions could be analyzed in greater depth.

Nonetheless, a chronological ordering facilitates a general but useful understanding of how Kenyan novelists have responded over the decades to the changing exigencies of Kenyan society, particularly to the rapid growth of the postcolonial city. We begin with the 1960s, the decade that gave birth to the Kenyan novel, and the decade that established significant precedents for the years that followed.

Chapter 2

The 1960s: First Generation Novels

While there were no authentically indigenous novels by the time of Kenyan independence in 1963, Kenyans had been writing and publishing in slowly growing numbers during the closing years of colonial rule. Most obvious was a developing critical mass of ethnographic and autobiographical writing, beginning with a study of Kikuyu traditions by the man who was to become Kenya's first president, Jomo Kenyatta. *Facing Mount Kenya* originated as Kenyatta's doctoral thesis in anthropology from the London School of Economics in the 1930s. Other nonfictional accounts also depicted traditional ways of life, the armed struggle against British rule, and the conflicts between Western education and traditional beliefs and ways of life. Their titles suggest their content: *Land of Sunshine: Scenes of Life in Kenya Before Mau Mau* by Muga Gicaru (1958), *Mau Mau Detainee* by J.M. Kariuki (1963), and *Child of Two Worlds* by Mugo Gatheru (1964). In the years leading up to independence, Kenyan writers were finding literary outlets for expressing and exploring their experience, even if these expressions were not yet in novelistic form.

Meanwhile, Makerere College in Uganda encouraged students to produce literature based on canonical Western models, resulting in a growing corpus of short stories and poetry. Kenyan students were involved with the production of East Africa's first literary journal, the Makerere student publication *Penpoint*, founded in 1958. David Cook's edition of *Origin: East Africa* (1968) anthologizes many of the early stories and poems from *Penpoint*. The independent journal *Transition*, begun in Kampala in 1961 under the editorship of Rajat Neogy, included literature and literary criticism along with essays on political and social issues. With this new growth in literary activity, it seemed inevitable that the production of novels was sure to follow, just as it had elsewhere in Africa.

As it turns out, Kenyans published only a handful of novels during the 1960s, but these works laid the groundwork for what was to become a flourishing genre. Two writers in particular—Ngugi wa Thiong'o and Grace Ogot—set the standards for the first generation, producing novels that were to inspire and influence the Kenyan authors who were to follow them. Ngugi and Ogot produced the archetypal characters in Kenyan fiction and set out the thematic concerns of their generation.

It is not overstating the case to assert that Ngugi (who, around 1970, stopped using his Christian name, James) single-handedly founded the Kenyan novel. His *Weep Not, Child* (1964), the first published anglophone novel from East Africa, was quickly followed by *The River Between* (1965) and *A Grain of Wheat* (1967). Ngugi also wrote short stories and plays during this era, including *The Black Hermit*, the first full-length anglophone play by an East African, which was performed at Makerere in 1962 but not actually published until 1968. Ngugi's development as a writer is in itself an excellent guide to the broader trajectory of the Kenyan novel. He initiated and defined the genre, both as an author and academician in Kenya as well as during his later experience in exile, and the novels he produced in the 1960s outlined the major preoccupations and aspirations of his generation in an unparalleled way. The radically new directions in his writing since that first decade, while criticized in many quarters, represent original and influential experiments that continue to shape the broader developments in Kenyan writing.

All of Ngugi's work has in common a preoccupation with Kenyan social and political issues, and we see in his writing an ongoing quest for the appropriate form in which to express those concerns. These preoccupations and concerns may be grouped in three broad and interrelated categories; if Ngugi is their primary representative during the 1960s, we also see them picked up and elaborated upon by the other novelists of his generation. The first of these preoccupations is a historical impulse: revisiting and reconstructing the region's past in order to understand the roots of independence-era Kenya. This impulse is closely linked to the phenomenon of ethnographic and autobiographical writing that preceded Ngugi's work, but translated into the form of the novel. The second category of concerns involves a critical assessment of the influence of imported, European forces on traditional, indigenous ways of life. Like their colleagues in other former colonies in Africa, Kenyan writers have been preoccupied with the problem of how society deals with the alienating influences of colonialism on the one hand and the growth of new, postcolonial forms of society on the other. Generally dubbed the tradition-modernity conflict, this phenomenon is so important, according to the Kenyan critic Chris Wanjala, that the response to alienation constitutes the defining characteristic of the region's literature. The third category involves social commitment in the arts. Ngugi, like others of his generation, demonstrates in his writing an urgent sense that cultural and artistic expression is not a sufficient end in itself, but rather must somehow be connected to political and historical reality.

These three concerns appear in all of Ngugi's novels from the 1960s, but each one corresponds in a particularly strong way to one of his three novels from that era. *Weep Not, Child,* for instance, has as its overarching theme the first of these concerns, the importance of understanding Kikuyu history in order to provide meaning in the present and direction for the future. The family of the child protagonist, Njoroge, lives as squatters on their ancestral land, now controlled by a British settler, Howlands, and a Kenyan collaborator, Jacobo. The three families highlight the broader history of the region, and in this novel Ngugi emphasizes, in an especially clear and effective manner, the historical themes that run through much of his writing—most notably a recounting of Kikuyu creation myths and legends, the history of land alienation that accompanied colonialism, and the significance of Mau Mau for the Kikuyu.

Njoroge, as the first in his family to attend school, hopes to help them to prosperity through education. Nevertheless, the text makes clear, he receives much of his most important education in the *thingira*, his father's hut, where the stories of Kikuyu history are passed on by his father to the children of Njoroge's generation. These include not only the creation story of Gikuyu and Mumbi (the Adam and Eve figures of Kikuyu legend) but also the more recent story of how Kikuyu land was appropriated by the British:

> Then came the white man as had long been prophesied by Mugo wa Kibiro, that Gikuyu seer of old. He came from the country of ridges, far away from here. Mugo had told the people of the coming of the white man. He had warned the tribe. So the white man came and took the land. But at first not all of it. (25)

After World War I, during which a number of Kenyans were pressed into service as part of the British Army's Carrier Corps, British settlement in the area increased. Many Kikuyu were dispossessed of their land, including Ngotho's family:

> My father and many others had been moved from our ancestral lands. He died lonely, a poor man waiting

for the white man to go. Mugo had said this would come to be. The white man did not go and he died a *Muhoi* [a landless "squatter"] on this very land. It then belonged to Chahira before he sold it to Jacobo. I grew up here, but working . . . (here Ngotho looked all around the silent faces and then continued) . . . working on the land that belonged to our ancestors. (25-26)

Njoroge's awareness of the history of his family and community grows steadily. Howlands, on whose farm Ngotho works, represents the settler presence while Jacobo, on whose land he lives, represents those Kenyans who collaborated with and benefited from British rule. The plight of the *ahoi*, "squatters" on farms that historically were their own, becomes a key concern in *Weep Not, Child*, along with the question of how best to respond to it. Njoroge's brother chooses armed revolution but ultimately fails; his father wavers between acquiescence, when he refuses to take the Mau Mau oath, and confrontation, when he joins a general strike. As with much of Ngugi's writing, the novel closes on a symbolically open-ended (and in this case, depressing) note. Following the death of his father and the capture of his brother, Njoroge is dissuaded from hanging himself only by his mother: "He saw the light she was carrying and falteringly went towards it" (135); but he is plagued by the shame of his impotence and cowardice.

The River Between was in fact the first novel Ngugi wrote, but it was published second. An exploration of history is also significant in this work, but subsumed within the conflict between old and new ways, between tradition and modernity. The novel highlights two key aspects of Kikuyu history in the colonial era: the importance of female circumcision as a rallying point for the resistance to colonial rule, and the emphasis on education through the formation of independent schools (67). The main conflict, however, is between traditional religious practice and the newly imported religion of Christianity.

Two ridges, Kameno and Makuyu, stand joined by the "valley of life" and the river Honia, "which meant cure, or bring-back-to-life" (1). The boy Waiyaki (from Kameno) and the girl Nyambura (from Makuyu) are brought together through school but kept apart by irreconcilable differences between their parents. Nyambura's father, Joshua, is a missionary convert who "always preached in sharp ringing tones that spoke of power and knowledge" (29). His born-again followers on Makuyu ridge find themselves in increasing opposition to Waiyaki's family and others from Kameno, who "remained conservative, loyal to the ways of the land" (28).

Matters reach a head when Joshua's second daughter, Muthoni, insists on being circumcised against her father's wishes. She represents the desire for a compromise between the ridges and the religious traditions they represent; Muthoni wants to be "a Christian in the tribe" (53), a symbol of the "river between" that could unite the ridges. Waiyaki also emerges as a mediator between these divisive forces, a reluctant hero who looks to education, through the establishment of independent schools, as a way to unite Kenyans and lead them to prosperity and autonomy. These attempts to overcome the hostility between the two camps are foiled by extremists on both sides, and *The River Between* closes, like *Weep Not, Child*, with a protagonist who is unable to overcome betrayal, impotent in the face of extreme social forces and beset by guilt.

A Grain of Wheat, Ngugi's third novel, is by far his most mature work of the decade, in both style and content. Leaving behind the child protagonists and colonial-era settings of his earlier novels, Ngugi takes a hard look at a key moment of Kenyan history—that uncertain time between its status as a colony and as an independent nation. *A Grain of Wheat* is the prototype for a later sub-genre of the Kenyan novel that might be termed disillusionment literature, stories that reflect a widespread disappointment with the failed promises of independence.

The protagonist is Mugo, whose name recalls the legendary Kikuyu hero, Mugo wa Kibiro, celebrated in Ngugi's earlier works. This Mugo, however, is an antihero, for while the village reveres him for his involvement in the independence movement, it becomes clear that his role in that movement and the circumstances that led to his eventual detention and torture are rather more ambiguous than the villagers realize. In fact, we discover, he betrayed the true hero, Kihika.

Ngugi's brilliant move in this novel was to depict not a hero of independence, but a traitor with a tender conscience, thereby presenting in an unusually complex way the many implications of the aftermath of the independence struggle in which families and friends were divided. We also see, as in all Ngugi's works, an integration of Christian and traditional religious imagery. The novel is replete with allusions to Christ figures such as Kihika, who always carried a Bible with him and ended up "crucified" (26), as well as to obvious Judas figures like Mugo. At the independence day celebrations, the leader of "one of the many independent churches that had broken with the missionary establishment" (217) gives the invocation, calling for the blessings of the God "who also created Gikuyu and Mumbi, and gave us, your children, this land of Kenya" (218).

As a result, *A Grain of Wheat* represents, even more strongly than Ngugi's earlier novels, the strain of socially committed writing that characterized the first generation of Kenyan writing. This is made clear in the novel's prefatory note. Whereas many authors take the opportunity to claim imaginative license, reminding their readers that what they are reading is a work of fiction, and that any resemblance to actual people or events is coincidental, Ngugi makes the opposite point. While it is a work of fiction, he asserts in his note, nevertheless "the situation and the problems are real—sometimes too painfully real for the peasants who fought the British yet who now see all that they fought for being put on one side."

Grace Ogot, the other significant Kenyan novelist of the 1960s, established her credentials with a series of short story collections and the novel *The Promised Land* (1966). Although Ogot has continued to write, her literary production fell off somewhat following her involvement in a political career. Her novel establishes several literary precedents: *The Promised Land* was the first work to be published by the East African Publishing House; it was the first East African novel by a woman; and it was the first Kenyan novel by a non-Kikuyu, in fact one of only two such novels published in the 1960s.

Ogot's novel is strongly anthropological, depicting and explaining a variety of Luo customs, such as marital expectations and obligations, the nature and importance of intergenerational relationships, and traditional beliefs about medicine, healing, and witchcraft. Like many early African novels, whose writers felt the need to explain local custom and practice, Ogot provides sufficient information for an outsider to understand the characters' motivations and decisions in light of their setting, but she does so in a particularly skillful way, avoiding overt didacticism and incorporating the material as part of the natural flow of her tale. Her interest in recording Luo history through literature is perhaps unsurprising, given her marriage to the Kenyan scholar and historian, Bethwell Ogot, to whom her first novel is dedicated.

The Promised Land has a good deal in common with Ngugi's novels in the way that the characters find self-knowledge through examining their traditions: The protagonist Nyapol and her husband Ochola break with tradition by emigrating to Tanzania, but it is clear that their identity and support comes from the Luo community to which they belong. If there is a difference, it is that Ngugi's novels, although local in content, contain nationally relevant political themes. Ogot's novel, by contrast, while international in its scope, is concerned primarily with politics on the local level, in this case a specific Luo community in Western Kenya and Tanzania. At the same time, *The Promised Land* does not directly address national political issues in the direct manner that Ngugi does. Europeans are peripheral in her text. Indeed, apart from the brief appearances of an English priest, who sexually harasses his female converts, and a European mission doctor, whose medicine is ultimately unable to heal Ochola, they are non-existent.

The marriage of Nyapol to Ochola, the eldest son of a relatively prosperous family, gets off to a shaky start when Ochola begins to entertain prospects of migrating from Western Kenya to Tanganyika. Against the wishes of Nyapol and the rest of his family, Ochola stubbornly forges ahead with the move, convinced by the stories of other emigrants that he will find greater wealth in Tanganyika, where the land is fertile and free for the taking. He meets with early success, but runs into trouble when his disgruntled neighbor, a witchdoctor who holds a grudge against the new wave of Luo immigrants, places a powerful spell on Ochola that causes him to break out in thorny warts. In the end he is healed, but he has to return to Kenya as a condition of his healing, leaving his land and belongings behind.

Ogot's novel highlights key social tensions in newly independent Western Kenya. Intra-Luo conflicts as well as the territorial disputes with other groups such as the Nandi are explicated in passages in which Ochola and Nyapol work on their land. More recent history is presented by a harpist aboard the steamer, who entertains travelers with a ballad about losing family members in the "white man's war" in Burma. In addition to the conflict between Ochola's desire to emigrate and his family's more conservative desires that he stay on the familial land as expected, there is also an incipient conflict between Western and African medicine.

One of the most memorable passages of the novel likens the new labor relations accompanying urban capitalism to witchcraft. In Kisumu, on their way to Tanganyika, Nyapol reflects on the new realities of wage labor as she sits waiting for the steamer, watching the dock workers. Her observations serve as an accurate foreshadowing of the results of Ochola (and others) blindly chasing after wealth:

> The sun was high in the sky and beat furiously upon the naked chests of the labourers. They were perspiring heavily and beads of sweat from their heads poured down their faces and mingled with those on their chest. Their worn out backs were white-washed with dust from the bags, while their once protruding bellies were now sunken.
>
> "Why waste your tears? The men have chosen the job themselves. They are neither slaves nor prisoners: they are just normal men who have come to town to earn money to buy things for their wives," explained Ochola, seeing his wife looking at the labourers and weeping for them.
>
> "Ridiculous! Only bewitched men could willingly choose such a job! A man whose wife is bewitched as well." (53-54)

In Nyapol, Ogot has created the Kenyan novel's first complex and powerful female character. We will see her influence in writers who followed Ogot, and, in the meantime, her actions raise a number of questions, implicitly and explicitly, about gender roles in traditional Luo society. When Nyapol's sister is harassed by Father Ellis, she has to hide the incident, since no-one "would marry a girl touched by a white man" (51). Even marriage is not satisfactory, Nyapol realizes in her bluntly insightful manner, since it is merely "a form of imprisonment in which the master could lead you where he wished" (46).

Of the other three novels published in the 1960s, two treat the Mau Mau experience. Charity Waciuma's *Daughter of Mumbi* (1967) features strong autobiographic and ethnographic components, but with sufficient imaginative content to classify it as a novel. The narrator presents a child's perspective on the Mau Mau conflict and the cultural syncretism of the Kikuyu population in relation to medical and religious practices. Godwin Wachira's *Ordeal in the Forest* (1967) also presents youths' perspectives on the era. In *A Calabash of Life* (1967), Khadambi Asalache has presented another strongly ethnographic novel, this one set among the Luhya. Like Ogot, Asalache demonstrates an interest in examining African history and recording African tradition.

As a group, the novels produced in Kenya during the 1960s were few but influential, tending to replicate the thematic concerns evidenced in Ngugi's early work. To varying degrees, all reconstruct the past either in order to preserve a record of disappearing traditions or in an attempt to understand the present through an analysis of history. All demonstrate the dilemmas of young protagonists faced with reconciling tradition and a changing society. All implicitly support the notion that literature should contribute to society by treating serious rather than frivolous issues. The regional origins of the writers are also reflected in their topics, with Kikuyu writers focusing on the Mau Mau experience and writers from Western Kenya, Ogot and Asalache, exploring other types of social conflicts. This first generation of novelists established a thematic repertoire that would resurface in the years to follow, albeit in expanded form. Ogot and Ngugi in particular would continue to write and influence the direction of Kenyan literature. The tentative first steps of the 1960s were about to turn into an avalanche of novels during the next decade.

Chapter 3

The 1970s:
Kenya's Literary Boom

The dramatic growth in Kenyan writing during the 1970s is readily quantifiable. Hans Zell's *Reader's Guide to African Literature*, a standard reference, lists nineteen entries from Kenya in its 1972 edition (covering the previous decade), seven of them novels. By contrast the *New Reader's Guide*, published eleven years later, includes more than one hundred Kenyan entries, of which two-thirds are novels, in addition to several dozen titles listed under the category of "popular fiction." Already in 1974, Douglas Killam could claim, inevitably referring to Taban's remark about East African literary barrenness, that "since 1966, the literary landscape of East Africa has changed quite decisively" (see Bruce King, ed., *Literatures of the World in English*, 117).

Numbers alone do not tell the whole story, of course. The 1970s also saw a qualitative improvement in the climate for East African art and imaginative writing. Creative and intellectual activity in East Africa was flourishing during this period, particularly in university communities. Writers and other artists saw themselves as part of a distinct and active social and cultural movement. In Nairobi, artists of all stripes met regularly at such downtown venues as Elimo Njau's *Paa ya Paa* art gallery or at the poetry and fiction readings organized by Marjorie Oludhe Macgoye at the S. J. Moore Bookstore, where she was manager. Book-writing competitions sponsored by the East African Literature Bureau (EALB) and the East African Publishing House (EAPH) provided incentives for new, younger writers. The artistic and literary community was gaining in strength and numbers.

New social and cultural periodicals had also appeared. *Transition*, the prestigious Kampala-based journal, inspired a host of other literary journals: the University of Nairobi's *Nexus* was founded in 1967, later to be replaced by *Busara* and *Mwangaza*; *Dhana* succeeded *Penpoint* as Makerere's literary magazine; *Darlite*, from Tanzania, became *Umma*; Oxford University Press began *Zuka: A Journal of East African Creative Writing* in 1967, while EAPH featured *Ghala*, a regular special issue of the *East Africa Journal* dealing specifically with literature. In addition to these and other scholarly publications, new general-audience magazines like *Joe*, *Trust*, and *Drum* included original local fiction and reviews of new literary works.

The appearance of these publications facilitated a growing critical mass of local literary criticism, culminating in a series of book-length critical studies in the early 1970s. Taban lo Liyong's *The Last Word* (1969) comprised the first collection of East African literary criticism, followed shortly by Ngugi wa Thiong'o's *Homecoming* (1972), Peter Nazareth's *Literature and Society in Modern Africa* (1972), and *Standpoints on African Literature* (1973), edited by Chris Wanjala.

Writers and critics of this time initiated a series of heated debates, discussing the relationship between African writing and the Western literary tradition. In 1968, Taban lo Liyong, Ngugi wa Thiong'o and Owuor Anyumba proposed replacing the English department at the University of Nairobi with a department of literature, making African writing, rather than

European writing, the core of the curriculum. In 1971, the University of Nairobi hosted a major event, the Festival of East African Writing, which, unlike the Makerere conference of a decade earlier, was predominantly regional rather than continentwide. At the festival, writers and critics debated the general direction of East African writing, including issues such as language, the writer's obligations to universal or local concerns, and African artists' use of traditional or Western models for inspiration. This era of creative ferment was, for many, exhilarating and fast-paced: "Each year is like a decade," proclaimed festival participant Bahadur Tejani (see Andrew Gurr and Angus Calder, eds., *Writers in East Africa*, 135). Finally, it seemed, Taban's lament was being hearkened and disproven.

Along with this interest in literary production, however, there appeared a concurrent and contradictory disillusionment with the failed promises of independence. Regional unity was dissolving along with the East African Economic Community; Idi Amin was rapidly dismantling the "pearl of Africa"; and Julius Nyerere was on the verge of making the unprecedented move of sending troops into a neighboring African country. The vibrancy of the University of Nairobi as the region's intellectual center came partly at the expense of Makerere University; Ugandan intellectuals sought refuge in Kenya and elsewhere following Amin's rise to power in 1971. In many arenas, pessimism was replacing the euphoria of the previous decade, and it was becoming rapidly apparent that the promises of independence were not being fulfilled for many East Africans.

In Kenya, the emergence of a new indigenous political and economic elite did not decrease the misery of the masses or the gross social inequities that were institutionalized under the colonial system; in fact, social inequality seemed only to be increasing. The term "neocolonial," coined to describe a situation where a few individuals within the ruling classes change but the basic social structures of the colonial era remain essentially intact and in some ways more entrenched than ever, seemed especially relevant. At the same time, the East African city, Nairobi in particular, was entering an unprecedented state of crisis thanks to a rapid growth in urban population at the same time that many of the social services available for that population were shrinking.

These contradictory developments constituted the social context for Kenyan writing in the 1970s, so it is hardly surprising that the Kenyan novel developed in various directions. The novels of this era can be classed into four distinct but overlapping categories: (1) historical novels, exploring colonial and pre-colonial Kenyan settings; (2) novels centered on the conflicts between traditional and modern ways of life, which began with the colonial encounter but intensified dramatically in the postindependence era; (3) novels of disillusionment, which underscored the betrayal of the hopes surrounding independence; and (4) most significant of all, urban novels, exploring the nature of life in the modern African city. With the exception of the urban novel, each of these thematic developments had models or prototypes in the first generation of Kenyan writing from the 1960s, but each was also elaborated upon and further developed during the writing boom that characterized the 1970s.

Works from the first of these categories, historical novels with colonial and precolonial settings, have as their literary antecedents the ethnographic and historical novels of Grace Ogot, Khadambe Asalache, and Charity Waciuma, as well as the nonfiction histories and ethnographies by Kenyatta and others. Like their predecessors, many of the historical novels from the 1970s feature a strong anthropological impulse, seeking to explore, explain and in many cases valorize traditional customs and beliefs.

What was new to the 1970s was the increased number and broader scope of these historical novels. Johnson Mbugua places his love story, *Mumbi's Brideprice* (1971), in a precolonial Kikuyu setting, while Lydia Mumbi Nguya's similar novel, *The First Seed* (1975), features Kikuyu-Maasai intergenerational conflicts. Abel Mwanga's *Nyangeta: The Name from the Calabash* (1976) also includes a romantic interest, although the text seems to be more interested in the precolonial customs of the Ebukwaya, the heroine's ethnic group in rural Western Kenya. J.C. Onyango-Abuje's *Fire and Vengeance* (1975) is a similarly ethnographic novel set among the Luo. Valerie Cuthbert takes the longest historical view of any anglophone Kenyan novel so far in *The Great Siege of Fort Jesus* (1970), a dramatized account of the victory of the Omani Arabs over the Portuguese in Mombasa in 1698.

Like Ngugi, Waciuma, and Wachira before them, the Kikuyu writers who treat the colonial era are primarily concerned with recording the Mau Mau experience. Two notable texts present the dilemmas of those Kenyans who chose not to participate in Mau Mau. The protagonist in John Karoki's *The Land Is Ours* (1970) has to choose between loyalty to the British authorities, who invested him with what little authority he has, and the Mau Mau movement. Edward Hinga's *Out of the Jungle* (1973) is about a man falsely accused of joining the Mau Mau rebels. Two of Meja Mwangi's early novels, *Carcase for Hounds* (1974) and *Taste of Death* (1975) dramatize the forest fighting between the rebels and British troops. It is instructive in this regard to consider David Maugham-Brown's insightful argument in *Land, Freedom and Fiction: History and Ideology in Kenya* (1985) that Kenyan writers, with the significant exception of Ngugi, demonstrate in their equivocal portrayal of Mau Mau the ideological ambiguity of the postindependence political regime, which tended to distance itself from the Mau Mau movement even as it tried to associate itself with the achievements of that movement. The Mau Mau novels of the 1970s certainly display that ambiguity.

In *Leave Us Alone* (1975), Samuel Kagiri deals with Mau Mau only obliquely, focusing instead on another key issue for the Kikuyu under colonialism: female circumcision. In a manner reminiscent of Ngugi's *The River Between*, Kagiri's novel presents a young woman's dilemma in deciding whether to proceed with the traditional ceremony, given the strong missionary teachings against the practice. Muthoni Likimani also recounts the conflicts raised by mission activity in Kenya in *They Shall Be Chastised* (1974), a novel that presents both positive and debilitating effects of mission activity upon the "chastised" African population.

Like Mugo, the flawed hero of Ngugi's *A Grain of Wheat*, the tragic personal shortcomings of the protagonists in many of these historical novels are magnified in the context of the internecine conflict and rapidly changing social structures that characterized colonial Kenya. Stephen Ngubiah's *A Curse from God* (1970) presents Karugu, a backsliding Christian convert whose troubles include bickering wives, alcoholism, and his arrest as a Mau Mau suspect. Karugu's problems are of a personal, psychological nature but are compounded by the conflicting messages he receives in his changing world. Muturi, a similar character from Daniel Ng'ang'a's *Young Today, Old Tomorrow* (1971), has little success in dealing with life after returning to Kenya following his work for the British forces in World War II. These novels show how, whatever else they did, the colonial experience and the resistance to it left a legacy of shattered lives and broken relationships.

A highly original novel in its historical vision is David Mulwa's *Master and Servant* (1979). This beautiful tale, unfolding in a timeless setting, is unique in its sensitive portrayal of traditional caste and family relations. Like Ngugi, Mulwa chose a child as the protagonist for his first novel. Young Joseph Kituku is sent to a strict and inhospitable school, where he has to board with the power-hungry friend of his father. Most interesting, though, is his growing relationship with Hamad, a servant with a mysterious background who becomes Joseph's real teacher and mentor. Throughout, the motives of the powerful and powerless, masters and servants of all stripes, are observed and commented on by the slowly maturing Joseph.

The second category of writing is also the most common during the 1970s. These are the novels that explore the tradition-modernity conflict in the postindependence era. Often structured as a *bildungsroman*, the typical plot presents a child or youth facing increasingly complicated decisions about how to reconcile (or choose between) family traditions and a new, "modern" reality, which is most often accessed through formal education. The stories may resolve in a more or less successful cultural syncretism, typically held together in the name of a national or transnational cultural ideal, but just as often they end in a complete breakdown and in cultural alienation. Unlike the historical novels, the anthropological impulse to explain tradition is subordinated to an exploration of the conflicts presented by tradition's encounter with modernity.

The most beautiful Kenyan novel of this type is Mude dae Mude's only novel *The Hills Are Falling* (1979), in which the protagonist experiences double alienation, first as an African entering a British education system, but then, even more importantly, as a member of a community that is marginalized within Kenyan society. Galge belongs to the pastoralist Gabra ethnic group from Northern Kenya and becomes the first student from remote Marsabit district to enter high school, eventually landing a Nairobi-based civil service job. The story's central dilemma is the dissonance that Galge experiences between the expectations of his family and his community on the one hand, and the completely different sort of life he must live and choices he must make as a government official living in Nairobi.

Alfred M'Imanyara's only novel treats similar dilemmas. Set in Mugweland, a fictionalized rural Meru, *Agony on a Hide* (1973) is the story of three generations of two families linked by marriage. In the first generation, Mutema, a leader in Fig Tree Village, has to deal with the military defeat of his community by the "ghosts" who have newly arrived in East

Africa. His daughter Wanja marries a convert and preacher of the new European religion who has high aspirations for his family and moves them to Nairobi. When their daughter Mparu is killed by a burglar, the villagers in Mugweland refuse to allow her to be returned and buried on her home soil, as required by custom. Throughout these tensions, Wanja continues to hear a "strange call"—an urge to "return to Fig Tree Village." Written in a simple but poetic style, M'Imanyara's story idealizes neither traditional nor modern society; rather, it explores the social tensions that appear in each.

The same dynamics appear in Rebeka Njau's *Ripples in the Pool* (1975), a highly symbolic story of the idealistic Gikere, who marries a prostitute and returns to the village in an attempt to leave the problems of urban life behind. The story closes with a murder near a pool guarded by an old man. If the peace of tradition has been shattered, it remains to see whether it is irrevocably so, or whether the ripples in the pool will eventually clear.

A character from another of Kenya's historically marginal groups, the Maasai, is the focus of a *bildungsroman* from Kenneth Watene. In *Sunset on the Manyatta* (1974), Nylo "Harry" ole Kantai is the only child from a rural Maasai family to be sent to school. He excels there and eventually ends up in Germany on a technical training program. The end result is ole Kantai's renewed appreciation for his nation and culture. He returns to Kenya determined to drop his Christian name and to "buy myself the largest Swahili dictionary there is" (263). Unlike Mude's text, which is a closer and more subtle examination of cultural difference as compounded by the various cultural groups within Kenya, Watene asserts a more general national and East African identity in the face of a generalized European tradition.

The Maasai writer Henry R. ole Kulet presents similar tales of cultural conflict in his first novels, *Is It Possible?* (1971) and *To Become a Man* (1972). In each, a young Maasai boy's schooling conflicts with his father's traditional way of life.

Ultimately, however, both novels suggest that a successful integration of the two worlds is in fact possible through balancing allegiances to both, but only when each is subsumed to a broader ideal of national, intertribal unity.

It should be no surprise that in many of these works formal education is the main catalyst for cultural conflict. Many of the earliest African novels, created by writers who themselves were among the first generation to be educated through the colonial system, focus on the conflicts that resulted from participation in this departure from traditional education. These are typical first novels for many African writers, including such canonical West African works as Camara Laye's *L'Enfant noir* (1953), Chinua Achebe's *Things Fall Apart* (1959), and Kole Omotoso's *The Edifice* (1971). In Kenya, this trend was encouraged by such publisher-led initiatives as the East African Literature Bureau's students' book-writing competition, since student writers naturally enough produced books that focused on the tensions resulting from formal education, as in Billy Ogana Wandera's *Hand of Chance* (1970) and Miriam Khamadi Were's *The High School Gent* (1972). An interesting work of juvenilia was produced by an entire girls' high school class when Butere Girls High School Form IVA collectively authored *Loice: High School Student* (1970). Like the child protagonists of Ngugi's early novels, the characters in these new works are most concerned with the ways that a formal education questions or clashes with traditional practices.

If the formally educated child is one of the standard characters to experience the tradition-modernity conflict, the other is the figure of the "been-to," someone who has returned from travel or study overseas (usually in America or Europe). In Henry Owino's *A Man of Two Faces* (1978), Okure is a been-to who, as the novel's title suggests, is unable to reconcile the person he has become with the person that his family and girlfriend knew him to be before he left. The personal and cultural conflicts drive him to an unfortunate end. In a similar vein, *The Girl from Abroad* (1974), by Sam Kahiga, examines what it means to fall in love with a been-to, in this case a woman who studies in the U.S. Tension arises between the new middle-class life that the protagonist Mbathia aspires to, symbolized most fully by his downtown Nairobi apartment, and his family who live in a semirural suburb.

A novel that combines romance, a colonial setting, the experience of the been-to, and the "return to Fig Tree Village" solution is Hazel Mugot's *Black Night of Quiloa* (1971), in which a romantic attraction serves as a metaphor for the broader seductive power of Western influence. Hima, a beautiful young woman from the coastal island of Quiloa, abandons her engagement to Abu and instead marries an Englishman and returns to his country. At first she is enamored of her new life and home (significantly, on Shilling Street), but soon comes to resent and eventually despise her "prison of ice." In the end, she returns to the warmth and security of Quiloa, and it is unclear whether the whole experience has merely been a dream.

Religion is a basic source of social conflict in many of these novels. Ngugi had already highlighted this volatile issue in the clash between the missionary convert Joshua and the traditionalists of Kameno Ridge in *The River Between*, but the issue clearly continues to concern writers a decade later. While some novels emphasize the destruction to traditional society posed by Christian missionary activity, others (such as Ngugi's early works) lament the unnecessary polarization created by religious conflict. Still others highlight the liberatory potential of Christian practice in the face of repressive political practice. An example of the latter is C. Okello's *The Prophet* (1978), published by Uzima Press, the publishing organ of the Church of the Province of Kenya (CPK—the Kenyan branch of the Anglican Church). In this story, a pastor is torn between ethnic affiliations and a Christian commitment to peace and justice. An unusual twist on the typical religious conflict appears in Sam Kahiga's *The Girl from Abroad*, mentioned above. In this case, the conflict is not between tradition and a new Christianity, but rather between a conservative Christian father and the secular, post-Christian ethics of the new professional class to which the son subscribes.

Novels of disillusionment, the third major category to emerge during the 1970s, portray the injustices and inequalities that have persisted since Kenya's independence. These novels highlight the harsh inequalities of modern capitalism, the corruption of the postcolonial elite, the betrayal of Mau Mau freedom fighters, and the failure of postcolonial governments to restore justice as manifested in, for example, the derailing of the various postindependence land resettlement schemes or the inability of the common person to resist exploitation by the new elite. The protagonists tend to be highly educated and underemployed, recent university graduates whose idealistic hopes for society have soured.

The first model for the disillusionment novel, Ngugi's *A Grain of Wheat*, suggests that the complex conflicts of interest that surfaced during the struggle for independence are likely to have effects after independence as well. With its hopeful ending, however, *A Grain of Wheat* is not as fully disillusioned as the texts that began to appear in the 1970s. The first and most important of these is Leonard Kibera's *Voices in the Dark* (1970), which as the title suggests presents a series of gloomy portraits of Kenyans from various walks of life who find themselves powerless and directionless following independence. *Voices in the Dark* is also significant as Kenya's first fully urban novel and will be discussed in more detail in Chapter Five.

Two other archetypal disillusionment novels of this era were written by Silvano Onyango Wambakha. *The Way to Power* (1974) is a biting criticism of nepotism, inefficiency, and corruption in the civil service system; although it is set in Uganda, the story pertains equally to the rest of East Africa. Chido and Mwele are both been-tos, meeting as students in the U.S. before returning to rural civil service postings after their studies. Chido is undoubtedly the more brilliant student,

the more competent administrator, and the more morally reso-
lute of the two. Mwele, who finally graduates from an American university after six years and several changes in his course
of study, uses ethnic and religious connections with those in
positions of political power to secure favorable posts and regular promotions, despite his incompetence. Although Chido is
the sort of person who deserves to be rewarded and encouraged, the focus of the story is mainly on Mwele and his transformation from an idealistic young person to being a greedy
exploiter of his own people.

Wambakha's second novel, *The Closed Road to Wapi*
(1978), is about the corruption inherent to political power.
Sanyo, a peasant from a rural area of a country remarkably
similar to Kenya, moves to the capital to look for employment
and housing, counting on the help of his uncle, Senator Simba.
An opposition politician, Simba began his career honestly,
committed to the socialist ideals on which the country was
founded, but power quickly corrupts him. His attempt to
maneuver a vote of no confidence in the government is overturned by the People's Democratic High Council, which uses
a loophole in the law to unseat its opponents and turn the
country into a one-party state. Sanyo, meanwhile, has been
unfairly ousted from his apartment. When he challenges the
move in court, it turns out that his landlord is none other than
his Uncle Simba, who bought the property from an Indian
whom he had managed to deport. Seeing the true nature of
his uncle's character, Sanyo hangs himself.

Ngugi's single novel from the 1970s is also an example
of disillusionment literature. A logical sequel to *A Grain of
Wheat*, *Petals of Blood* (1977) is set in postindependence
Kenya, in the fictional Kikuyu community of "Ilmorog, our
Ilmorog." The repetition of this formula, with its plural pos-
sessive, highlights the communal consciousness that perme-
ates the narrative point of view. The story poses as a murder
mystery, opening with the interrogation of suspects in the as-
sassination of the directors of the Theng'eta Brewery. We

come to know four main characters: a headmaster, a barmaid, a trade unionist and a shopkeeper. The real hero of this story, however, is the community of Ilmorog itself. The nature of Kenyan society becomes clear to them following an epic march on Nairobi, during which they learn the traitorous and corrupt nature of their politicians and business leaders. Put together, the titles of the four sections of the novel—"Walking," "Toward Bethlehem," "To Be Born," and "Again . . . La Luta Continua"—invoke the historical vision found in William Butler Yeats' poem "The Second Coming," but with a twist. The new-born beast, presumably, is the neocolonial society dominated by capitalist lackeys like the directors of the brewery, but the addition of Amilcar Cabral's call for a continued struggle ("*La luta continua*") suggests that Kenyans should not give up in their efforts to reform their society and shape their history.

Frequently, novels of disillusionment are also urban novels, the fourth category of Kenyan writing to emerge in the 1970s. Beginning with Kibera's *Voices in the Dark*, Kenyan writers suddenly began to focus their attention on the topic of life in the modern African city, a shift that was so significant and so all-encompassing that it may be considered the single most outstanding development since the inception of the Kenyan novel. In the city, novelists were to discover both the site and symbol for their major preoccupations. For many, the city was the ultimate example of all that had gone wrong since independence. In the lives of Nairobi's slum children, Meja Mwangi, Thomas Akare, and others found ample ground for urban picaresque drama. Others, like Charles Mangua and David Maillu in their popular thrillers, found much to celebrate (albeit sometimes paradoxically) in the bustle, activity, and fast pace of urban living. Because of its great significance, this phenomenon will be dealt with in more detail in Part Two.

In all, the 1970s saw the Kenyan novel come into its own. If there are inconsistencies and even contradictions in its development, this should not be surprising given the inconsistencies and contradictions of Kenyan society itself. Most importantly, unlike the previous decade, Kenyan novelists of the 1970s could write with the sense of having a small but significant novelistic tradition, and they began to elaborate and expand on the repertoire of themes as presented by Ngugi, Ogot, and others. Kenya's literary boom era was about to come to a close, however, and again it is Ngugi who offers the instructive individual example of what was happening to Kenyan writing as a whole. His arrest, detention, and eventual exile are the most publicized and obvious examples of the restrictions under which Kenyan writers were to operate as the 1980s began. These restrictions by no means put an end to Ngugi's literary production, of course. Similarly, Kenyan writers as a group, having established a full-blown literary tradition, would continue to work—despite the odds.

Chapter 4

The 1980s and 1990s: The Post-Kenyatta Era

The death in 1978 of Kenya's first president, Jomo Kenyatta, provides a convenient historical marker in our chronology of the country's literature. What we find is that the brief literary boom of the 1970s was followed by a sudden decline in the overall quantity of Kenyan published works in the post-Kenyatta era. The publication of novels especially decreased dramatically in the 1980s and 1990s. Kenyans had published an average of eleven new novels each year from 1970 to 1979, but in the ensuing decade that average was cut in half, and in the early 1990s new novels continued to appear at the lower rate of four to five per year. As a whole, Kenya's publishing industry "reached its peak in 1976 with a high output of new titles and an export turnover almost equivalent to that of imported raw materials" (J.S. Musisi, *African Publishing Review* 1:2, June/July 1992, 9). The high point for novels, in sheer numbers at least, was 1975, when 20 new titles were published. In the years following Kenyatta's death, the situation changed dramatically. In 1982, R.N. Ndegwa was already noting in his annual bibliography of East and Central African literature that "since 1978 this region's literary output has been diminishing at a considerable rate" (*Journal of Commonwealth Literature* 17:2, 1982, 2). While still well above the pre-1970 output, this nevertheless represents what might be called, in Tabanian terms, a return to drought conditions in the literary landscape.

Kenyan novelists in the post-Kenyatta era have faced a number of significant obstacles on various fronts. One of the most important has been a paucity of publishing outlets. Although Kenya compares favorably to its neighbors in this regard, with Nairobi serving as the most active publishing center in the region, the options for novelists have declined in recent years. Four major private publishing houses dominate the post-Kenyatta era: Oxford University Press, Longhorn (formerly Longman Kenya), East African Educational Publishers (EAEP, formerly Heinemann East Africa), and Macmillan. These are supplemented by two parastatal publishing boards, the Kenya Literature Bureau (KLB, formerly the East Africa Literature Bureau) and the Jomo Kenyatta Foundation, as well as church-sponsored publishers such as Uzima Press, Baptist Publishing House, and Evangel Publishing House. During the 1970s most of these groups, as well as the East African Publishing House (EAPH), a nonprofit organization overseen by the East African Cultural Trust, actively produced fiction of all types.

Since then, however, many of these outlets have been closed to novelists. In the mid-1970s, EAPH folded, and the organization that succeeded it, Transafrica Publishers (founded by EAPH's erstwhile head John Nottingham), lasted only a few years. Oxford University Press decided against publishing fiction as a matter of policy. The Kenya Literature Bureau has not produced a novel since 1985, and the Jomo Kenyatta Foundation has only one copublished novel to its credit. The major players in fiction remain EAEP and Longhorn, but their production of novels in the 1990s has fallen dramatically. Across the board, publishers admit, the emphasis at all the publishing houses, including the parastatals, has been increasingly on educational texts, since these represent sure sales and profits. In addition, few Kenyan publishers have distribution arrangements that allow them to market local publications internationally.

The market for Kenyan publications dropped off considerably when trade with Tanzania was halted in 1977, following the final collapse of the East African Economic Community. Economic considerations are important in a more general sense as well: Kenya's brief economic boom of the mid-1970s, concurrent with the expansion in literary output, gave way to a steady decline in overall economic performance that nose-dived in the early 1990s. The novel, historically a form that owes its success to the development of an educated leisure class with disposable time and income, is likely to suffer during an economic crisis, and this has certainly been the experience in Kenya. A further ongoing dilemma for writers is Kenya's low literacy rate, which also limits readership.

Finally, censorship and self-censorship due to political considerations have certainly limited the production of novels during this era. Beginning in the late Kenyatta years and throughout Daniel arap Moi's presidency, writers were regularly incarcerated and a number of high-profile artists, including Ngugi wa Thiong'o, Micere Mugo, Koigi wa Wamwere, and others, went into exile. These cannot have been encouraging developments for any budding Kenyan novelists.

Nevertheless, the decline in literary output during the post-Kenyatta era could not erase the fact that by this time Kenyan writers had established a significant national literary tradition on which a new generation could build. If the 1980s and 1990s saw fewer novels published overall, the new works that did manage to appear were characterized by two healthy trends: a deepening and continued exploration of established themes and ideas on the one hand, and an impressive creativity in presenting new material on the other.

Novelists in the post-Kenyatta years have continued to elaborate the thematic categories established by their predecessors. The appearance of historical and anthropological works set in colonial or precolonial Kenya, for instance, demonstrates that Kenyan writers have not yet exhausted the topic. Colonial-era Mombasa is the setting for Hammie Rajab's *Rest in Peace, Dear Mother* (1982), in which the protagonist confronts the ghosts of his family history on his own wedding night. Grace Ogot returned to the novel with her recounting of *The Strange Bride* (1989), the translation of a Luo myth earlier published as *Miaha* (1983). David Macharia's *The Smasher* (1984) presents internecine religious strife among the precolonial Kikuyu that is reminiscent in many ways of Samuel Kagiri and Lydia Nguya's works. Valerie Cuthbert's *Dust and the Shadow* (1990), like her first novel, treats a subject from early Kenyan history, this time about a migratory people in the Rift Valley who are searching for a home in the mythical land of Ophir.

Similarly, Kenyan novelists of this era seem to feel that more remains to be said about the Mau Mau experience: Sam Githinji's *Recovering Without Treatment* (1981) is about friends who are divided by the Emergency (the colonial administration's response to the Mau Mau crisis); and Samuel Kahiga examines the movement's hero yet again in *Dedan Kimathi: The Real Story* (1990), a fictionalized account told from the perspective of a female participant. An idealistic solution to racial conflict appears in Mwangi Gicheru's fifth novel, *The Mixers* (1991), a moral tale set in central Kenya during the decades preceding independence: The settler community is scandalized when Victor Robinson marries his Kikuyu house-servant Lillian, starting a "mixer" family.

Familiar themes related to the tradition-modernity conflict also resurface regularly in the post-Kenyatta novels. Significantly, many of these works come from writers who do not belong to the Kikuyu or Luo communities, perhaps because Kikuyu and Luo writers had already explored these themes or, more probably, because the social tensions accompanying modernization were becoming more relevant for other, traditionally more peripheral groups: Stephen Kiyeng's *Echoes of Two Worlds* (1985) is the first novel to present a Kalenjin protagonist; the Maasai writer Henry ole Kulet continues his exploration of how to reconcile ethnic and national allegiances in *The Hunter* (1986), *Daughter of Maa* (1987) and *Moran No More* (1990); and Maurice Mumba's *The Wrath of Koma* (1987) is a colonial-era story set among the coastal Mijikenda, containing a warning against forsaking traditional values.

Although disillusionment novels continued to appear, it is difficult to gauge how the decrease in literary production and the increase in literary censorship may have affected the production of these types of works. These are, after all, the works that are most likely to disturb the political establishment. In any event, "disillusionment novel" may no longer be the most accurate term for this type of writing. "Disillusionment" implies a betrayed idealism that has largely disappeared following the death of Kenyatta, who, as a historical figure, was inextricably linked to Kenyan independence. Thirty years later, novelists are less likely to be mourning a loss of hope and more likely to be writing works of social criticism in general. "Novels of political critique" might be a better term to apply to more recent works of this type.

The most biting works in this category come from Ngugi wa Thiong'o, whose *Devil on the Cross* (1982) and *Matigari* (1989) were published after he went into exile. Other works highlighting the corruption of the postcolonial political and economic elite are Sam Githinji's *Struggling for Survival* (1983), which portrays the breakdown of traditional morality and the betrayal of a cooperative land redistribution scheme, and Mwaura Waweru's *The Siege* (1985), in which the protagonist is persecuted for trying to organize farm workers. Grace Ogot's *The Graduate* (1980) revisits the formula of the trials of a been-to.

Urbanization has continued at a rapid pace in the post-Kenyatta years, and urban novels continue to dominate Kenyan writing. Some, like Thomas Akare's *The Slums* (1981), emulate the picaresque tales of Nairobi's underbelly in the manner laid out by Meja Mwangi's urban trilogy. Others, like Marjorie Macgoye's *Street Life* (1987), present impressionistic vignettes reminiscent of Leonard Kibera's *Voices in the Dark*.

Not all urban novels are critical, of course. Yusuf Dawood, Pat Wambui Ngurukie, and other popular writers celebrate the lives and exploits of the urban middle and upper classes. In fact, if any type of writing has flourished in the post-Kenyatta era, it is popular writing, the primary difference from the previous generation of popular texts being its contemporary content. David Maillu published an updated revision of his blockbuster *After 4:30* in 1987. Two thrillers—*Black Gold of Chepkube* (1985) by Wamugunda Gateria, and *The Border Runners* (1984), coauthored by James Irungu and James Simanyala—are based on the coffee smuggling from Uganda that was rampant during the "coffee boom" of the 1970s. AIDS appeared for the first time in Kenyan fiction in Gateria's second novel, *Nice People* (1992). Inspired at least in part by *Washington Post* reporter Blaine Harden's article about Kenya's AIDS epidemic, the sensational story includes dilemmas in medical ethics, the controversy over sex education in Kenyan schools, and the widespread notion that "nice people" are not at risk of acquiring the disease. Meja Mwangi's popular works from this era also allude to contemporary issues like apartheid, wildlife conservation, and the Ethiopian famine in the mid 1980s. Overall, the clear bestseller of this period was the first-person adventure tale, *My Life in Crime* (1984) by John Kiriamiti, written in the style of Charles Mangua's popular prototype *Son of Woman*.

While all these works elaborate the now-established formulas and categories of Kenyan writing, the most interesting developments in the post-Kenyatta years involve works that offer formal or thematic developments that are either totally new or that offer significant original twists to the established patterns. A number of these works—most notably from Marjorie Oludhe Macgoye, David Maillu, and Meja Mwangi—

will be discussed in Part Two, since they are best treated as examples of urban literature. For the moment, however, it is worth looking briefly at innovative new works from five other writers—Ngugi wa Thiong'o, Koigi wa Wamwere, Moses Ndissio-Otieno, Wahome Mutahi, and Francis Imbuga—all of whom refined and reshaped the character of the Kenyan novel in the 1980s and 1990s.

It is fitting that Ngugi wa Thiong'o, always the single most dominant force in Kenyan literature, is also influential in the most recent novelistic trends. In Ngugi's case, this has to do with the increased overtness of his political message, which appears in his fiction and nonfiction alike. Ngugi's novels of the 1980s have been criticized for their direct ideological messages—messages that some critics see as coming at the expense of the finer aesthetics and artistry of his earlier pieces. These later works are, the argument goes, simply too polemical and too specifically directed to a particular situation to be of lasting interest. Whether one considers this overt politicism a strength or a weakness, it is certain that Ngugi has produced the most unambiguously political works in all of Kenyan literature. Even though his novels of the 1960s were fundamentally informed by political concerns, and even though *Petals of Blood* and his plays in the 1970s also moved in the direction of overt political commentary, in *Devil on the Cross* (1980) and *Matigari* (1989) Ngugi attacks the Kenyan economic and political establishment in an unprecedentedly direct way. That directness is enhanced by Ngugi's use of rhetorical strategies from orature and his historic decision not to write in English; technically, these are not anglophone novels, since both are translations from Kikuyu originals.

Devil on the Cross is an allegory of postcolonial political and economic corruption. The heroine Wariinga, who has managed to overcome the early interruption of her education (after she had become pregnant by a rich "sugar daddy"), finally lands a secretarial job in Nairobi, but she returns to her home in Ilmorog when a new set of troubles begin. She is fired for resisting her boss's sexual advances; her boyfriend, a university student whom she had supported with her salary, drops her now that "the grade cow has stopped yielding milk" (25); and her landlord evicts her when she protests a rent increase. When she arrives in Ilmorog, Wariinga attends a "feast of thieves and robbers," who turn out to be local capitalists and businessmen celebrating their abilities to exploit their fellow Kenyans. This is the beginning of a new social awareness for Wariinga.

The story satirizes Kenyan capitalists in a series of hilarious parodies. The "thieves and robbers" compete in their extravagant boasts of how they have enriched themselves through trickery and injustice at the expense of the Kenyan people. Because their convocation includes guests from Europe, America, and Japan, only those who have reached international standards of thievery may be included in the competition:

> stories of people breaking padlocks in village huts or snatching purses from poor market women were shameful in the eyes of real experts in theft and robbery, and more so when such stories were narrated in front of international thieves and robbers. (95)

The testimony of the land speculator Gitutu wa Gataanguru (whose vision for the future includes controlling and selling air), Kihaahu wa Gatheeca (who bribes his way into a political position that he uses to further enrich himself), Mwireri wa Mukiraai (who goes too far in suggesting that Kenyan capitalists might eventually become independent of their international counterparts), and Nditika wa Nguunji (who is a smuggler) are wildly applauded by the convocation participants.

Although these exploiters are the obvious target of Ngugi's attack, the novel is also critical of those who allow these frauds to be perpetrated upon themselves. As one contestant announces:

> I'm very grateful to the masses of the Kenyan people.
> For their blindness, their ignorance, their inability to
> demand their rights are what enable us, the clan of
> man-eaters, to feed on their sweat without their asking
> us too many awkward questions. (117)

Devil on the Cross is the story of Wariinga's gradual coming
to political consciousness. She begins to understand the nature of her own misfortunes and the interconnectedness of her
personal, sexual, and economic exploitation. Realizing that
she can no longer be a passive observer, Wariinga takes deci-
sive action: in a dramatic showdown, she shoots the Rich Old
Man from Ngorika (her erstwhile "sugar daddy" and father of
her new fiancé) and walks out, aware "with all her heart that
the hardest struggles of her life's journey lay ahead" (254).

The novel is unique in the directness of its message as
well as the narrative style that Ngugi adopts. The pistol shots
at the end are like the book itself: a direct and unequivocal
response to contemporary Kenyan society. *Devil on the Cross*
forces the characters and the readers into a clear ideological
choice, either to take action against the corrupt status quo or
to acquiesce by their inaction. One must either join the "clan
of parasites [or] the clan of producers" (53).

For Ngugi, this ideological choice includes the artist's
medium of expression. *Devil on the Cross* was the first novel
Ngugi wrote in Kikuyu, a move that would have been applauded by his character Gatuiria, the university professor who
befriends Wariinga: "Let us now look about us. Where are
our national languages now? Where are the books written in
the alphabets of our own languages? Where is our literature?" Gatuiria asks (58). Not only the language, but the form
is crucial. Just as Gatuiria is seeking the right form for a genuinely indigenous musical composition, so Ngugi is seeking an
authentic national identity for the novel. The result is a story
based on the shape and rhythm of oral storytelling. The novel
is introduced by a *gicaandi* player, a self-proclaimed "Prophet
of Justice." The complex structure of the novel imitates much

from orature: stylized characterizations, repetition, frequent use of song. Understanding and guidance toward liberation, it is suggested, may be found in the traditional music and literature of a people.

Devil on the Cross is clearly written for a Kenyan audience, since it includes meticulous references to landmarks in Nairobi and Nakuru and on the matatu ride to the fictional town of Ilmorog. Contemporary events and problems are explained through the use of traditional proverbs and stories, such as the story of Kamoongonye, a Gikuyu ballad in which a young woman rejects marriage to a rich but old man in favor of the poor, young Kamoongonye. There is an implicit critique of the popular trends in Kenyan fiction in an allusion to the novels of "James Hadley Chase, Charles Mangua and David Maillu" (17) and in the formulaic rhetoric of the Sugar Daddy stories. When Boss Kihara speaks, it is a parody of popular literature easily recognizable to anyone who has read Mangua, Maillu, or any of the popular Spear Books titles:

> Beautiful Kareendi, flower of my heart. No one but you can type [my letters]. For I want to send them care of the address of your heart, by the post of your heart, to be read by the eyes of your heart . . . . I beg you, don't write *Return to sender*. (21)

The final solution in *Devil on the Cross* is ultimately an individualistic one. If collective action is alluded to, Wariinga's final action is a solitary one. This is the main difference between *Devil on the Cross* and Ngugi's sixth novel, which is also overtly didactic but emphasizes the need for collective action. *Matigari*, like its predecessor, attacks capitalism and its local practitioners as the source of Kenyan ills, and it also calls for direct, armed action as the appropriate response to the situation. But it is clear that any resistance or change can only be effective if it results from a communal effort. Even the protagonist himself represents a group of characters: the name Matigari ma Njiruungi, "the patriots who survived the bullets" refers to the Mau Mau fighters "and their political offspring" (20).

When Matigari emerges from fighting in the forests, he replaces his gun with a "belt of peace," but he is shocked and dismayed at the situation he finds. Although Kenyans are now running the country, the legacy of oppression and injustice continues. His quest for truth and justice highlights the lies and propaganda promulgated by the government's "Ministry of Truth and Justice." The solution, Matigari concludes, is group action on the Mau Mau model. He resolves to

> go to all the public places, blowing the horn of patri-
> otic service and the trumpet of patriotic victory, and
> call up my people—my parents, my wives, my chil-
> dren. We shall all gather, go home together, light the
> fire together and build our home together. Those who
> eat alone, die alone. (6)

Even though Matigari himself disappears at the story's end, swept away in a river while pursued by the authorities, the child Muriuki takes up his struggle by returning to the forest and digging up his weapons. As with all of Ngugi's work, the conclusion is open-ended, suggesting that the story is just be-ginning. In this case, a new generation must deal with Kenya's social ills, however using the same tactics of communal resis-tance applied in fighting colonial rule, i.e., through Mau Mau.

A rather similar work, although oddly enough it appeared as part of the Spear Books series of popular novels from Heinemann, is Koigi wa Wamwere's *A Woman Reborn* (1980). Like Ngugi, Koigi has been vocal in opposition to govern-ment policies, and, like Ngugi, he was detained and exiled; *A Woman Reborn* was written on toilet paper while the author was in Nairobi's Kamiti Prison. The short work presents the life stories of two characters: Njooki Kimeria, the wife of a business tycoon, and Wahome, a poor teacher and tutor of their children. When Kimeria is killed in the midst of some shady smuggling business in Uganda, it precipitates a long evening of reminiscing and soul-searching. Wahome reflects on the injustices that are allowed in the name of class, recalling for the benefit of the reader how his girlfriend committed suicide when her wealthy father refused to permit their relationship to continue because of his low social status. Njooki, whose story is treated at greater length, reflects on the betrayals by a series of men during her life. The novel ends up as a powerful statement in favor of women's emancipation, equating that struggle with the general struggle for justice of all Kenyan people.

As Njooki looks back on the behavior of her dead husband, her reflections become a litany indicting Kimeria but also Kenya's postcolonial "thief and robber" economic elite (as Ngugi might put it) as a whole:

> He added fuel to the fire by behaving even more disgustingly, this time politically.
> He supported the killing of those politicians who fought for the rights of the people.
> He supported the detaining of those Kenyans who fought for the democratic rights of the people.
> He supported and practised the sacking of workers who fought for higher wages and better working conditions.
> He supported the arrest and imprisonment of poor innocent people. (69)

Although it is on the surface a brief and fast-moving tale that fits the popular category characterizing Spear Books, *A Woman Reborn* is clearly no *Sugar Daddy's Lover*. The political message is loud and consistent, the allegory obvious. Njooki, who marries Kimeria partly out of necessity and partly because she is fooled into believing his promises of security and prosperity, symbolizes the Kenyan people in a broad sense. Importantly, however, she represents a people that, upon the death of the father figure—surely a reference to Kenyatta's death in 1978—is finally able to soberly evaluate that relationship. Wahome is surprised that Njooki drops the facade of mourning as soon as all the visitors have left, replacing her black with "a red and black striped skirt and a light green polo neck" (2)—the national colors of the country. By the end of her tale, he wonders aloud at how Njooki could have "learnt so much in her thirty years in this topsy-turvy world" (71).

Significantly, in addition to a sober reflection on her experience, artists—in this case, musicians—are the ones who have helped Njooki understand herself. Against her husband's wishes she listens to "records that sang the bitterness of people" (69), including the popular Daudi Kabaka and Joseph Kamaru. The ending, like Ngugi's *A Grain of Wheat*, is a hopeful one, with the promise of a new dawn following Kimeria's death.

Ndissio-Otieno's first novel, *A Blurring Horizon* (1991) also contains an implicit critique of postcolonial corruption but in a far more subdued and introspective style. The novel is unique among the Kenyan corpus in its focus on complex individual psychology. The novel in fact poses as a detective story, beginning with a double murder aboard the Kisumu-Homa Bay steamer, but it is about much more than a mafia-style killing, as internal psychological action dominates the work. The narrative is framed by the funeral of Ochieng', an ambitious young man who works his way into businesses in Homa Bay and then Nairobi. In a series of complex flashbacks, we are introduced to the power struggles within the companies where Ochieng' works, his relationship to his girlfriend Lilly, and their daughter Caroline. Like other protagonists in his position, Ochieng' has to balance the expectations of his extended family with his own aspirations in all these areas.

Ochieng's story highlights the moral dilemmas of corporate business in Nairobi, the difficulty of balancing modern and traditional lifestyles, and issues of religious syncretism. The "blurring horizon," where Lake Victoria's waters meet the sky, fascinates the child Caroline and provides the novel's title, but it also points to the uncertainties of balancing all these issues for someone like Ochieng', as well as problems that constitute the child's future. What is noteworthy about *A Blurred Horizon* is the subtle merging of complex symbols like this with an examination of the characters' psychology. Unfortunately, the book is marred by frequent stylistic and technical problems, which most likely result from the fact that it is a vanity press publication. It only wants a competent editor.

The most successful appropriation of the popular novel to transmit a serious message comes from Wahome Mutahi, whose two novels rely on satirical humor to tell the grizzly tale of the treatment meted out to Kenyan political dissidents. Mutahi is probably best known in Kenya as the creator of the popular humor column, "Whispers," in the Nairobi newspaper *Sunday Nation*. The same wry sense of humor in the face of life's hazards and injustices is present in *The Jail Bugs* (1992), which, despite its serious topic, is unrelentingly funny. When Albert Kweyu accidentally runs into a child with his car one Sunday morning, it leads to a detention in Wakora Wengi ("many thugs") prison. *The Jail Bugs* is the story of the regular beatings, inedible food, lice, and unsanitary conditions of prison life, and is without doubt the most interesting example of the "prison tale" subgenre of Kenyan writing, perhaps because it is based on Mutahi's own fifteen-month experience in Kenyan prisons. The novel is critical of Kenyan society in general, suggesting that life on the Nairobi streets may be even worse than prison, thanks to scant employment opportunities and the uncertainties of life in Nairobi slums.

Mutahi's earlier novel, *Three Days on the Cross* (1991), is a less polished but equally unsettling story that alludes to the detentions surrounding the Mwakenya scare of the 1980s, when the Kenyan government claimed to have uncovered an underground movement (called Mwakenya) committed to its overthrow. In the novel, Albert Momodu, a bank director, and the journalist Ogundipe Chipota are wrongly implicated as members of the "July 10 Movement," a group bent on unseating the "Illustrious One," who rules a fictional and un-named country that bears an uncanny resemblance to Kenya. The two men are locked up when Momodu's wife, unhappy about his bar-hopping habits, tells her priest of her problems; the priest informs the police, who arrest the two men. They spend three days being tortured in jail, since the police are under pressure from the Illustrious One to produce conspira-tors who will confess to plotting his overthrow. When they realize their mistake, the police decide the only thing to do is kill the men and leave their bodies to the hyenas of Nairobi Game Park. As in his other novel, Mutahi's unique trait in *Three Days on the Cross* is his ability to tell a story of abso-lute corruption with a heavy dose of irony and humor.

One of the more experimental new novels comes from Francis Imbuga, who is best known for his active involvement in Kenyan drama as an actor, director, and playwright. The publication of *Shrine of Tears* (1993) is of special interest because even though it is Imbuga's first experiment with the novel, the overriding concern in this narrative is the condition of dramatic arts in contemporary Kenya. The novel, set in the fictional nation of Kilima, focuses on the role of theater and other art forms in the dissemination of national cultural val-ues. The conflict surrounds issues of who in fact controls events at Kilima's National Theater, who has access to pro-ductions (either as participants or as spectators), and the ex-tent to which the Shrine (as it is called in the novel) is or is not in fact a "national" institution. In the process, the text high-lights the contradictory roles of universities, university stu-dents and faculty, politicians, expatriate "experts," the police force, and traditional cultural practices in producing a national culture.

If Imbuga's works are not as overtly ideological as Ngugi's, they do contain clear critical commentary about postcolonial East African politics and society. The title of a study of Imbuga's works by the Ugandan playwright John Ruganda neatly sums Imbuga's tactics: "Telling the truth laughingly" is Imbuga's way of criticizing authority and getting away with it, Ruganda suggests. His texts allow the targets of his criticism to save face by avoiding direct attacks and by a liberal use of humor. Imbuga participates in the trickster tradition, telling the truth in the face of authority but in a manner that depends on "the survivalist principle . . . that good art must protect itself from vilification, and its creator from incarceration" (*Telling the Truth Laughingly: The Politics of Francis Imbuga's Drama*, xxi).

Those familiar with Imbuga's plays will see many of his characteristic dramatic elements in *Shrine of Tears*: There is the issue of how to appropriately incorporate traditional with nontraditional practices; characters are awakened to their moral condition by the subconscious world of dreams, visions, and voices of dead friends; and there is an ambiguous ending, leaving it unclear as to whether or not the status quo will prevail. There is even a play within the action, although the politician for whom it was intended, the corrupt Minister of Culture, Hon. Gasia, fails to arrive.

Imbuga's first-hand experience with international representations of East Africa in film, most recently in *Gorillas in the Mist*, and his discomfort with the cultural dynamics they represent, feature prominently in the novel. Throughout, the concern is with "decolonizing the spirit," as the mentor character of Headmaster puts it, a reference to and a step beyond "decolonizing the mind" that Ngugi wa Thiong'o has emphasized.

In *Shrine of Tears*, Imbuga is also experimenting with form; this is the first self-referential Kenyan novel. We discover that one of the characters and narrators, Headmaster, is also writing a novel whose title is, curiously enough, *Shrine of Tears*: "I have been toying with this whole idea of writing a novel that would teach itself," he tells Boge. "A novel that would actively participate in its own interpretation" (184). Imbuga's is the first (and to date only) Kenyan novel to exploit this *mise-en-abyme* device.

Headmaster (a largely autobiographical figure) is the inspirational mentor for a new generation of up-and-coming Kiliman artists who face opposition on two fronts: resistance from the Kiliman political establishment on the one hand, and pervasive European cultural influence on the other. The story is about the struggle to recover, create, and nurture a genuinely Kiliman cultural identity in light of this opposition. The main actors in this struggle are the new university graduate Jay Boge and his dynamic girlfriend Luta Kanaya. When Kanaya is killed in a freak accident near a Nairobi construction site (an incident based on the tragic, real-life death of the University of Nairobi student Stella Muka in 1982), Boge is jolted out of his lethargy, since she represents the cultural spark that Kilima is lacking.

The social criticism in *Shrine of Tears* is much more direct than in Imbuga's plays. The epigraph notes that,

> There comes a time
> When an unspoken truth turns
> Against its keeper
> And silences him forever.
> That is why in *Shrine of Tears*
> Sits a little truth from our
> Not too distant past.

The novel is consequently much more direct than Imbuga's plays, almost to the point of didacticism. Even though there are plenty of lighthearted moments, the truth that is told is not always presented laughingly.

In the novel, the city is the primary site of this struggle for cultural identity. The geography of Kilima's capital in *Shrine of Tears* is a clear recreation of Nairobi:

> The Kilima National Shrine sits trapped between the National Broadcasting House to the north, the National University to the west and the large multinational Five Star Hotel to the east. To the south squats the City Police Headquarters. If it stood up and leaned slightly

> backwards, the main building of the police station
> would rub its shoulders with those of the administra-
> tive block of the National University ....
>
> To the northwest of the Shrine, peeping shyly
> through the gap between the University Library and
> the National Broadcasting House, stands the old Brit-
> ish Council building, sometimes simply referred to as
> the Cultural Centre by those who know what it means
> to be brief (2).

Those familiar with Nairobi will immediately recognize the
University of Nairobi, the Voice of Kenya broadcasting facilities, and the Norfolk Hotel. The Shrine itself is of course the
Kenya National Theatre, the "nerve center of white and more
recently, Asian cultural activities" but where "black Kiliman
cultural groups are effectively kept off by the prohibitively
exorbitant hire charges" (3). *Shrine of Tears* questions the
claims of the institution to be a center for *national* cultural
activities and asks how a genuinely national culture might
emerge in a place like contemporary Kenya, particularly in
light of the other institutions whose proximity so obviously
demonstrates the vectors of economic and political influence
surrounding the National Theatre.

The critical message of *Shrine of Tears* succeeds in large
part because it carefully avoids a simplistic scapegoating of
any particular group: Not all Europeans are evil, not all politicians are corrupt, and not all police are malicious. There are
dirty old white men like Silverspoon (80), but there are also
genuinely caring Europeans like the matron Clare Walker (62);
there are self-centered and greedy politicians like Gasia and
Mbagaya, but there are also upright MPs like the Minister of
Education and Natural Resources, Hon. Kamande (165); although the police may be involved in incidents like roughing
up Kanaya's feeble grandmother, which causes her death (145),
others are careful to help ordinary citizens like Boge (115).
Except for Headmaster and Kanaya, no character is perfect.
Boge, meanwhile, is a flawed hero in the tradition of Leonard

Kibera's Gerald Timundu: He drinks too much and is paralyzed because his idealism is countered by a deeply cynical attitude that prevents his taking action.

The model citizen is like the young woman Kanaya: well-rounded and accomplished in both engineering and the arts. The model society is one in which merit and achievement are fairly rewarded: Kanaya, we learn, has like most Kiliman artists been compensated inadequately for her work (100), and Headmaster has yet to receive payment for an award that he won for his contribution to national arts. The model for national culture has tradition as the source of its inspiration, but tradition is also carefully evaluated and aspects are rejected where necessary. At Kanaya's funeral, for example, her father insists that she be buried under the *mugumo* tree, a site normally reserved by tradition for the men of the family:

> The days of boys and girls are gone. Elders, those days are gone. The days that we now have in Kilima and elsewhere on this earth are days of children, not of girls or boys. (135)

Kanaya herself is primarily a symbol, standing for a new type of woman and a new type of country. She represents the future in which a new generation of young Kilimans redefine the way men and women relate to each other.

The ultimate message of *Shrine of Tears*, however, is that the birth of a new respect for Kiliman culture must grow out of a sense of self-respect and confidence of each of its citizens. The source of this self-respect, the text shows, is tradition on the one hand and the creative imagination of Kiliman artists on the other. As Kanaya tells Boge from beyond the grave, "*You* are the shrine" (153).

The city is the site where this new fight for cultural awareness must be waged, since it is in the city where the cultural and artistic imagination of Kiliman artists is most successfully squelched. Kilima's capital is where political control of creative expression is most blatant, where foreign cultural influence and foreign values are at their strongest, and where the lack of access for Kiliman citizens is most obvious—particularly in the symbol of the Shrine.

Within this bleak cityscape, however, are occasional glimmers of creativity that are the source of hope. The dreary Hell's Gate Bar and Restaurant has on its walls a mural whose artist is unknown and whose message is ambiguous, but that demonstrates the latent creative talent of Kilima. At Kanaya's funeral, the unemployed, teenaged hangers-on are another example of untapped creative talent:

> As I stood there watching this group, I remember wondering what excuse the Kilima Broadcasting Corporation had for not tapping such rich talent for their local radio and television programs.(136)

And, of course, there is the creative potential of the mentor Headmaster and the young university students like Jay Boge that has also gone unrecognized.

The city, clearly, needs to be reclaimed through the struggle of the creative imagination. But the outcome of that struggle remains in the balance at the end of the text. Boge and Headmaster have been roughed up by the police after a confrontation with Gasia and, as in Macgoye's *Coming to Birth*, we do not know what the outcome will be. The good matron Clare Walker assures us that "the young man will be alright" (229), but there is still no word about Headmaster.

In addition to its ambiguous ending, there are other significant ambiguities that *Shrine of Tears* does not fully address. One has to do with the role of money and international capital in postcolonial Kilima. Clearly, funding is a major problem for Kiliman artists, who at regular intervals have to resort to impromptu fundraisers to support their activities. Meanwhile, in the background are oblique references to the vast wealth of the city that is controlled by a very few, such as the "man of office stealing much-needed foreign currency from his motherland with a single telephone call" (226), a problem that is presented but never resolved.

The other dilemma is how to combat the colonized cultural spirit of Kilima in a strategically effective manner. The model of Headmaster, who lives a simple but comfortable life, fails to address the issue conclusively. Headmaster's answer seems to be that one must tell the truth—but, as in Imbuga's plays, one must know how to do it laughingly and know when to stop. The two primary truth-tellers in *Shrine of Tears* are Kanaya's grandmother, who stands up to the politician Mbagaya, and Boge himself. The former is killed, and, at the novel's end, Boge's fate is unknown. Clearly, truth-telling in Kilima can be a hazardous undertaking.

Part II

Urban Obsessions,
Urban Fears

Chapter 5

Postcolonial Urban Geography: The Evolution of Nairobi

At the time of its publication in 1970, Leonard Kibera's *Voices in the Dark* represented a fundamentally new development in Kenyan literary history. This was the first novel to be set entirely in the city and the first to treat the city as a complete microcosm, a world unto itself that stands for what Kenya *is* rather than merely an aspect of Kenyan society. Where earlier works offered the city as an important but undeveloped and always distant symbol, Kibera's Nairobi is the symbolic *sine qua non*—the essence of postcolonial society, or the crucial part that stands for the social whole.

The text is structured as a collage of characters and voices; many are entirely new to Kenyan fiction. At the heart of the story we encounter one such character—the "lonely boy," a nameless street urchin—who was to become a staple of Kenyan fiction following the appearance of Kibera's novel:

> Where the Public Street meets the street of the rich the
> lonely boy sits huddled against a shop of plenty. It's

well past midnight and since the reverend left, he too has been praying for rain, in between wondering how much longer he can hold out. Barefooted, ragged and able, he is the kind that bored policemen take as a specimen of disorder and lately the Reformatory Department has taken his picture no less than three times. He cannot help feeling a little famous .... He takes a light, from the breast pocket of his khaki shirt. It's one of those free matches that fold and carry a lot of loud writing in full colour. This one tells him in full exactly where to go if he is stranded in Europe next summer. So with dignity but stranded on this pavement he adjusts his hat and begins smoking under neon lights that advertise pork. Summer—is that not when all Europeans are stranded in Nairobi? (101-102)

The main concern in *Voices in the Dark* is the betrayal in postindependence Kenya of the individuals and ideals that motivated the resistance to colonial rule. In addition to the lonely boy, the novel features erstwhile freedom fighters who have been reduced to begging on Nairobi's streets, a collaborationist priest who has grown quite well-to-do and self-righteous following independence, and the protagonist Gerald Timundu, a cynical and disillusioned playwright who dropped out of university as a result of his frustration with being taught such irrelevant trivia as how eighteenth-century English gardens are different from nineteenth-century gardens. Gerald, who worked as a clerk for the multinational Pineapple Juice Company until he was sacked for his outspoken criticism of the company's unjust practices, is now composing his third play. His girlfriend, Wilna, is the daughter of a leading Nairobi businessman. Gerald's tale is framed by that of the former freedom fighters, Irungu and Kimura, who fought with Gerald's father in the Mau Mau struggle but are now beggars. Theirs are the most obvious voices in this dark city, opening and closing the book, but we also hear others. One of the most significant is Mama Njeri, Gerald's mother, who was a tough freedom fighter in her own right, even if she herself never hid in the forests. After her husband's death, she moved to the city with her son when their land was appropriated by the colonial collaborator Reverend Muroki.

Voices in the Dark uses urban geography to highlight the competing interests that are to be found in postcolonial Nairobi. The narrative jumps spasmodically between various key spaces in Nairobi's landscape: Gerald's small house in a secluded suburb, the alley frequented by Irungu and Kimura, the street where the lonely boy languishes, the "shops of plenty" that he can huddle against but never enter, the university, the church, a restaurant. Etisarap Road is the one space where all the voices overlap amidst their coming and going. Nairobi itself is a wasteland in this text, starkly inhospitable, and, above all, dark. The novel raises the crucial question about why those who struggled and sacrificed in the fight for land and freedom have been denied an adequate space of their own after independence. The novel concludes pessimistically, with the various voices expiring quietly or anticlimactically: Irungu's voice fades slowly away as he dies in his alley, while Gerald is shot dead in an offhand, parenthetical passage.

Voices in the Dark generated a great deal of critical attention after its publication, but has essentially been ignored since. Kibera's technique earned some admirers, who hailed his break from "the enthralling rules and formalities to establish his own style, creating new symbolisms and neologisms" (Fulgent Wanjohi, "Individualistic Symbolism in *Voices in the Dark*," *Busara* 4, 1972, 71). The style is impressionistic, with the plot subordinated to the creation of a mood, which is established by the collage of overlapping voices. The book also found detractors, who suggested less accurately that Kibera "lacks sincerity; he is merely adventuring with the pen" (Paul Njoroge, "Sincerity and Modern East African Writing," *Dhana* 1, 1971, 49).

In fact, the novel is a highly successful adventure that deserves to be ranked among the major milestones in Kenyan writing. Critics immediately noted that *Voices in the Dark* invokes the Fanonian model of the national bourgeoisie as a relatively powerless intermediary for international capital (Henry Indangasi, "Fanonist Overtones or Voices in the Dark?" *JOLISO* 1, 1973, 61-66). The text is reminiscent of the South African writer Alex La Guma's *A Walk in the Night*; Chris Wanjala described it as "the most serious novel to come from East African since [Ngugi's] *A Grain of Wheat*" ("Lonely and Diminished Men," *Busara* 3, 1971, 64).

The publication of Kibera's novel only slightly anticipated a veritable barrage of urban fiction, which has since come to dominate Kenyan writing. By contrast with the pre-1970 novels, in which the city was either ignored or (more frequently) treated as a foil for wholesome rural values, in the post-1970 novels the city became the regular setting. Novelists were finding in the city the site and symbol for their concerns. Life in modern, urban Africa became a new and ubiquitous theme in Kenyans' narrative repertoire.

Suddenly, everyone was writing about the city. Charles Mangua, famous for his role in initiating the Kenyan popular genre (to be examined in Chapter Six), quickly produced two urban adventure stories: *Son of Woman* (1971) and *A Tail in the Mouth* (1972). Marjorie Oludhe Macgoye's *Murder in Majengo* (1972) features urban intrigue in Kisumu. Mike Mwaura's *The Renegade* (1972), George Kamau Muruah's *Never Forgive Father* (1972), and Mwangi Ruheni's *What a Life!* (1972) all present specifically urban dilemmas for their citified characters. These works, coming immediately after Kibera's, signalled the opening of the floodgates for the new wave of Kenyan novels of the city.

One of first critics to comment on this new trend, Eleanor Wachtel, suggested in "The Urban Stereotypes of Urban Life in Kenya" (Institute for Development Studies, Working Paper No. 172, 1974) that although the urban novel was a more recent development in East Africa than elsewhere on the continent, it was likely to prove equally significant. Furthermore, she claimed, these types of novels are unparalleled in their ability to reveal the dynamics of African urban life, and observers of that life—such as the social scientists at the University of Nairobi's Institute for Development Studies, to whom her paper was addressed—would do well to pay attention to the urban novels. Wachtel was quite correct on both counts. Urban characters, settings and conflicts have dominated the Kenyan novel ever since. Kenyan writers began to draw from the city a whole new set of symbols, as cars and buildings, Western clothing, commercialism and commodification became the new signifiers of the ambivalent glamour of the city. The new Kenyan political and economic elite, with its power consolidated in the city, provided a whole new set of characters to explore.

It bears emphasizing that these characters and symbols are complex and often ambiguous. Slums, wretched and miserable as they are, also contain life. Posh hotels, glamorous as they are, can be cold and artificial. Cheap bars, encompassing and representing all the sins of city life, can also provide a sense of community and belonging in an alien environment. As we shall see in Chapter Eight, this ambiguity also applies to gender roles: Despite the numerical dominance of men and the common perception that the city prostitutes *all* of its inhabitants, the city can also offer women positive alternatives to the patriarchal social organization of rural areas. The most successful novels exploit and explore these ambiguities.

What may be deduced from a place where the concerns of its writers are overwhelmingly urban even though its population is predominantly rural, as is the case in Kenya? It seems insufficient to argue that simply because Kenyan writers themselves have found an education, a livelihood, a publishing industry, and even a readership in the city that consequently they will write so unrelentingly about it—although these factors certainly constitute part of the picture. There are three other key factors to be considered. First, the appearance of the urban novel at this particular time seems a logical result of the city's growth in importance; in 1970, as we shall see, Nairobi was facing a crisis of unprecedented proportion. Second, because the city is where the social conflicts and problems of contemporary Kenyan society are most clearly focused, Kenyan writers naturally found it a fruitful vein to mine. Finally, the novel as a form lends itself quite easily to the hybridity that characterizes the postcolonial city and consequently makes a useful literary vehicle for exploring urbanization. Understanding these phenomena, however, requires an appreciation of the nature and history of urban development in the region.

Unlike the East African coastal strip, where a number of important population centers were established as early as the first century, there were no precolonial cities as such in the Kenyan interior. There was, however, an existing spatial system organized around what historians refer to as "central places" or "exchange points" that served administrative, trading, social, or defensive purposes. These included caravan towns that were established as part of the long-distance trade routes at the end of the eighteenth century, as well as marketplaces for trade within and between communities.

When the British moved into the East African interior, they laid out an additional and entirely separate spatial grid; their administrative stations were generally located away from the already existing "central places," either for convenience or for health considerations. Missionaries established a third spatial system, generally locating their mission stations away from both the existing central places and the administrative centers, and usually featuring schools or hospitals. Consequently, at the beginning of the twentieth century the area now known as Kenya was characterized by a trifaceted, nonintegrated spatiality—precisely that sort of geography that Waiyaki observed as a child in Ngugi's *The River Between*.

The building of the Uganda Railway was the single most significant development in this region at the turn of the century, as it overlaid and altered irrevocably the emerging spatial structure mentioned above. Originally envisioned as a way of facilitating trade with Uganda (which until 1902 included what is now part of Western Kenya), and as a preemptive move against German territorial pretensions in greater East Africa, the tracks also opened up the Kenyan interior to European settlement. As in most early European imperial quests, economic exploitation of the area had at first been delegated to a private company, in this case the Imperial British East Africa Company (IBEAC), which was granted a royal charter in 1888. However, the capital investments required—specifically, the construction of the railway from Mombasa to Uganda—were too large for IBEAC, and the British state became directly involved, declaring Uganda a crown protectorate in 1893 and granting British East Africa (as Kenya was then known) the same status in 1895.

The railhead reached *enkare nairobi*, the Maasai name for this "place of cold waters," on 30 May 1899. A settlement emerged on this swampy area between the highland to the north, inhabited by an agricultural Kikuyu population, and the Athi plains to the south, inhabited by the pastoralist Maasai. Two months later, the railway administration headquarters was moved to the site and in 1907—despite opposition from various quarters, but on the urging of the railway administrators—Nairobi replaced Machakos as the capital of British East Africa. The railway became the backbone of the new colony, with Nairobi its central point.

More than most cities, Nairobi offered a perfect opportunity for colonial authorities to experiment with urban planning. Nairobi's design was the result of two predominant and not necessarily conflicting imperatives: on the one hand to create a model of the Garden City, a concept that was becoming important in British urban planning at the end of the nineteenth century; and on the other hand to create an essentially European city in the African setting, based on the South African model.

Although Europeans never formed much more than ten percent of Nairobi's population, the colonial administration maintained tight control of the city through a combination of residential zoning restrictions and pass laws. Racially distinct areas of town were built into the original design, with the railway officers' quarters clearly separated from the "native" housing, which was in turn distinct from the Indian bazaar area. The early planning commissions—the Williams Report of 1907, the Simpson Report of 1913, and the Feetham Report of 1926—recommended explicitly racial segregation as the basis for city planning. As Nairobi grew, a strikingly polarized residential pattern developed, with spacious white areas in the north and west, the densely populated Africa sections to the south and east, and the Asian areas serving as a sort of buffer in between.

Because Africans were only considered temporary residents of Nairobi, workers were generally not allowed to bring their families to the city. This resulted in an overwhelmingly male urban population. As workers migrated to the city in increasing numbers, Africans were initially allowed to live in "satellite villages" outside of the city center. Colonial authorities, who soon deemed these uncontrolled settlements to be problematic, became reluctantly but increasingly involved in organizing housing for Africans in Nairobi.

The Nairobi City Council had long relied on policies of containment and demolition of African settlements, under the assumption that providing more housing would only attract more people to the city—an undesirable prospect, in its eyes. As early as 1901, municipal authorities tried to control "squatters" by passing a law that allowed the forcible removal of "unauthorized" people. When this was deemed unsatisfactory, "native" villages were established in 1919 in Parklands, Kileleshwa, Ngara, and Pangani; in 1923 the authorities bulldozed the locations of Kaburini, Maskini, Mombasa, and Pangani, moving the residents to the "model village" of

Pumwani, today the site of one of the largest of Nairobi's slums.

A major change in housing policy began at the end of World War II, as the government policy of neglect and containment was replaced with a more deliberate policy of government paternalism. The city began to make provisions for workers to live there with their families, thus creating, beginning in 1939, the first housing estate projects for Africans in Ziwani, Kaloleni, and Pumwani. Others followed in the 1940s in Ofafa, Maringo, Makadara, and Jericho.

By the time of independence in 1963, Nairobi had been established as a tightly controlled and racially divided city. This carefully constructed geography would influence and limit urban development in the postindependence decades as well. What changed most in the 1960s, however, was the liberalization of colonial control on movement into the city, allowing a sudden growth spurt in Nairobi's population. Although rapid growth has characterized Nairobi throughout its 100-year history, the rate of urbanization increased dramatically through the late 1960s because immigration restrictions were lifted upon independence. The "squatter" settlements, a perennial thorn in the side of colonial authorities, mushroomed as slums in Kibera, Pumwani, and the infamous Mathare Valley grew significantly. By 1970, it was becoming obvious that urbanization was far outstripping the city's social services, infrastructure, housing, and employment opportunities. By 1970, it was clear, Nairobi was in a state of crisis.

One result of crisis in evidence today is that instead of being the uniform garden city originally envisioned, Nairobi is a city of dramatic contrasts. Because contrasts can be aesthetically pleasing, the Kenyan tourism industry has eagerly embraced this aspect of Nairobi; brochures, postcards, and other tourist literature favor the juxtaposition of the wild and exotic with the modern. Not all the contrasts are pleasant however. Most obvious is the huge discrepancy between rich and poor: "lonely boys" still huddle against shops of plenty;

well-dressed Nairobians in suits and ties pass beggars in rags; street children sniff glue in the alleys behind banks and tourist hotels; parking "boys" help Mercedes Benz owners find places for their cars in the congested downtown. Nairobi's residential structure continues the segregation established under colonialism: The northern and western suburbs are low-density, high-income areas, while the southern and eastern areas house a high-density, low-income population. The multistoried residences of the rich with their large gardens and high fences set a striking contrast to the large urban squatter settlements. The businesses and office buildings of the formal sector contrast sharply with the informal sector workshops and kiosks.

Many of these contrasts are the result of Nairobi's hybrid culture. This hybridity is evident on all levels of the social formation, but its basis on the economic level is most obvious in the coexistence of two separate but importantly linked spheres: the formal and informal sectors. The latter term first came into use following a major study of Kenyan employment by the International Labor Organization (ILO) in 1972—about the same time that Kenyans were exploring the very same phenomenon in their urban novels. In examining Kenya's employment statistics, the ILO mission discovered that because conventional studies concentrated on wage-earners in large or established firms, they were overlooking a large segment of the population that was making a living in small-scale, low-wage occupations that, for lack of a better word, were termed informal.

On closer examination, the ILO noted, the informal sector includes not only petty traders, hawkers, and shoe-shiners, but also carpenters, masons, tailors, cooks, taxi drivers, and other industrious workers supplying a wide range of goods and services to a large but poor segment of the population. The informal sector is characterized by ease of entry, as opposed to formal sector activities that often require education, skills, special training, connections, or capital. It uses indigenous resources, is family owned and quite small in scale—in contrast to the reliance on imports, corporate ownership, and the large scale of the formal sector. It is labor intensive, using skills acquired outside of formal schooling, and it is totally unregulated.

This lack of regulation is one of the reasons that the informal sector also typically operates under debilitating restrictions. Unable to control and tax these enterprises, the government and the formal sector see it as a threat and treat it accordingly. Furthermore, the difficult circumstances in which the informal sector operates often make it an eyesore: Because of their limited access to capital, these enterprises are located in poor areas of town, often in temporary facilities, and their products often do not conform to established standards.

A further reason for the harassment of the informal sector is ideological. Standards and codes for housing, construction, and businesses that were instituted during the colonial era required a sizable capital investment, such that small entrepreneurs were effectively shut out of industry and business. Following independence, the government was reluctant to lower the standards, since it would imply that Kenyans did not require (or desire or need) the same quality of homes, workplaces, or other facilities as Europeans. This would have created a set of double standards: one for Europeans, one for Kenyans. Consequently, because complying with building codes and other facility requirements often necessitates the use of imported rather than local construction materials, out of the reach of many Kenyans, the so-called informal sector is frequently compelled to operate illegally.

Official restriction and harassment of the urban informal sector was based on a number of false assumptions. First, it was assumed that informal workers comprised temporary or occasional migrants, who could be easily convinced to return to the rural areas. In fact, most "squatters," who make up the majority of these workers, are long-term residents. Second, it was assumed that informal workers were unemployed or only sporadically employed, contributing little to urban income, whereas in reality a vast majority (95 percent) are steadily employed, earning incomes in the informal sector that are in many cases quite large. Finally, it was argued that improving the living conditions and facilities in the informal sector would only increase migration to the city, and would therefore prove to be self-defeating. The solution was to make this life as unattractive as possible, thereby discouraging further migration to the city.

In addition to the ILO study, a second sociological analysis sheds further light on Nairobi's urban crisis. Andrew Hake's analysis of Nairobi in *African Metropolis* (1977) was groundbreaking when it first appeared and remains one of the best definitive studies of the city. Hake describes Nairobi as "two-faced," having a modern facade but with an increasing number of people in its backyard—the slums, shantytowns, and uncontrolled settlements, as they are variously termed. Life in these marginal areas is difficult for residents, who are vilified by the popular press and politicians alike as lazy, criminally inclined, and a drag on national development efforts. Eviction, harassment, and general insecurity and instability are a part of life for many. Hake, however, prefers the term "self-help city" to describe this sector. Like the ILO, Hake believes that it should not be seen as a liability but rather as having great potential for creative development.

It can hardly be a coincidence that at the same time that the ILO, Hake and others were making their studies of Nairobi's increasing urban problems, writers were also addressing the same issues. The new urban novels, from Kibera and others, were also pointing to the two-faced nature of Nairobi—to the desperation but also to the opportunity that may be found in the city. Because of this two-faced reality, Kenya's urban novels often appear contradictory in their messages, with some works celebrating the drama and activity of city life, while others condemn the very same things. The narratives demonstrate the city's attraction and repulsion; characters may be obsessed by its bright lights and glamour or fearful of its seductive dangers. In some works, the city appears as a carnival or playground, while in others it is equated with either parasites or prostitutes.

Novels that celebrate the city are generally popular works. While many of them feature moralistic endings—suggesting that despite the long celebration of the city's easy virtues that the reader has just seen, one really ought to settle down and lead a pure and sober existence—such didactic conclusions generally ring hollow. After all of Dodge Kiunyu's exciting adventures in Charles Mangua's *Son of Woman*, for instance, it hardly seems likely that he will settle down to a law-abiding retirement, despite his earnest protestations to that effect. Similarly, the abundant stories of successful criminals in the "my life in crime" subgenre of Kenyan popular writing are hardly negated by the conclusion typical to most of them (such as John Kiggia Kimani's 1994 novel, *Prison Is Not a Holiday Camp*) that "crime doesn't pay." In fact, as these works show, the extralegal activities of city life can not only pay quite well, they can be quite exciting at the same time.

Perhaps because of its hybrid nature, the city is a carnivalesque space in the Bakhtinian sense, a place where accepted social norms are temporarily inverted or suspended. Spectacle and performance are central to carnival, and Nairobi is above all a performative space. The officially sanctioned spectacles of football matches and political rallies, the hype of the Safari Rally, or conferences at the Kenyatta International Conference Centre are counterposed to and complemented and mocked by nonsanctioned spectacle. The lunch hour in Nairobi is a particularly performative moment, as sidewalk entertainers cajole and entertain the noontime crowds. Uhuru Park, a favorite grassy lunch spot, becomes a multiring circus, with circles of onlookers surrounding performers in various spots. Among the more popular sights are acrobatic and contortionist performances by young boys, some of whom have

have gone on to more established careers with the Kenya Acrobatic Company.

The most prevalent figures, however, are from Nairobi's major proselytizing religions, Christianity and Islam; these are the numerous street evangelists, who offer preaching at the level of performance art. Gesticulating and pacing, often with interpreters adding to the effect, sometimes supported by singing groups and musical instruments, their distorted microphones shriek competitive amplification. Jeevanjee Gardens is the performative space of choice for Nairobi's evangelists: On a typical noon hour every available space of this city block-sized park fills with competing preachers. Macabre spectacle is also common in Nairobi: mob justice, necklacing (in which a burning tire is tossed around a victim's neck), and the occasional forced circumcision receive reproving but sensational coverage in the local press.

Unreal space spawns unreal language. Today's Kenyan youth speak *sheng*, a catch-all term for the varieties of street slang that mix English, Swahili, and vernacular languages with newly coined terms. In a city where personal space is at a premium, *sheng* is a means of creating a linguistic space. Hip and hybrid, one of the primary functions of *sheng* is to serve as a code language, shutting out especially the older generation. Like any argot, as soon as the code is cracked, as soon as the terms are understood by outsiders, the language shifts.

Acrobatics and *sheng*, physical distortion and hybridity, make an excellent set of twin metaphors for urban culture. The postcolonial city, it has suggested, can be understood through its "street buzz," which is the sound of a chaotic clash between old and new, power and impotence, poverty and ease (Allessandro Triulzi, "African Cities, Historical Memory and Street Buzz" in Chambers and Curti, eds., *The Postcolonial Question*, 1995). While many of the urban novels celebrate this chaos in plot and theme, only one—the novella *Without Kiinua Mgongo* (1989) by David Maillu—has attempted to recreate the very language of hybridity. While the work is not written in true *sheng*, being rather a macaronic mixture of Swahili and English, and while the storyline is formulaic (a millionaire's daughter marries the son of the gardener), this short work must rank as one of the more interesting experiments from an already innovative writer.

The chaos that constitutes Nairobi is also a source of fear and danger, and many of the urban novels take the city as symbol of the threats to society. Nairobi as parasite is one of the most common metaphors in this regard. Just as some economists have suggested that the urban centers are a drain on the rural sector, many writers suggest that they are degrading the moral and cultural life of the country. Etisarap Road, the site of most of the action in *Voices in the Dark*, is itself an anagram for parasite, suggesting how we are to view the city. Another common metaphor is the city as prostitute, and the common appearance of this figure—in popular and serious works alike—is most often intended to suggest how we are to view urban realities.

Whether celebratory or critical, what we see above all in the new urban novels, and indeed in practically all Kenyan writing, is that postcolonial society is a hybrid place where various traditions encounter one another with results that are often explosive but more often left in an uneasy and unresolved state. Postcolonial reality is a contested reality, and the postcolonial city features a contested geography. To illustrate this conflict, novels regularly turn to characters from Kenya's new political and economic elite. No matter how they are portrayed, as objects of criticism or praise, these groups inevitably find the source of their power and influence in the city. Regardless of their origins or where they end up, these characters must pass through Nairobi—via its educational or economic or political institutions—if they are to wield wealth and power.

Most novels criticize the elite, showing them as either neocolonial puppets, callously rejecting the roles and obligations of tradition, or as power-hungry megalomaniacs drunk with wealth and prestige and in the process bringing the country to ruin. Like the city, they themselves are parasites. Ngugi is among the most direct writers in this regard; his most recent novels are indicative of a widespread skepticism in postindependence Kenya—a belief that the *samaki mkubwa* (big fish) holds all the cards and that as the system is presently set up, even a change in leadership will make relatively little difference to the country, since whoever is in power will simply take the opportunity to "eat." Eating as a symbol of corruption is especially appropriate in East Africa today, where food is scarce for many and where a large girth is taken as a sign of prestige, wealth, and power, giving rise to such stock characters as the landlord Tumbo Kubwa ("big belly") in Mwangi's *The Cockroach Dance*.

Along with this criticism of the elite, however, goes a fascination. The lives of the rich and famous are the stuff of popular stories the world over; readers are at once scandalized and enticed by the decadence and opulence of entertainment and political figures. In the same way, many of the popular Kenyan novels spend a great deal of time simply describing the hotels, resorts, and game parks that are the playgrounds of the rich and of tourists, but are impossibly expensive and inaccessible to most Kenyans. David Duchi's *Assassins on Safari*, for example, features elaborate descriptions of Amboseli Game Park between murders and chase scenes.

This fascination may simply reflect a writer's own class background and biases. Yusuf Kodwavwala Dawood, for example, is the most widely read Kenyan writer of Asian descent, having been raised in India and Pakistan and trained as a surgeon in England before establishing a successful practice at Nairobi's Aga Khan Hospital. Since the early 1980s he has published a regular "Surgeon's Diary" column in the *Sunday Nation*, where he recounts anecdotes from his surgical career. Many of these anecdotes made their way into his autobiographical reminiscences *Yesterday, Today and Tomorrow* (1985) and *Off My Chest* (1988). The tone and content of these autobiographical accounts are remarkably similar to those of his novels, which are also episodic in structure, featuring the hospitals, medical personnel and issues with which Dawood is well acquainted. What all of Dawood's works have in common is a distinctly conservative outlook on issues of gender and class. All center on urban lives and problems.

Dawood's most ambitious novel, *Water Under the Bridge* (1991), traces the history of three families (one Asian, one Kenyan, and one European) through three decades of Kenyan history. The story chronicles many of the important changes—the water under the bridge—that occurred in Nairobi during the thirty years following independence. Dawood is particularly interested in exploring race relations and attempting to show how "the prejudices of the sixties and seventies had disappeared" (327), giving way to a tolerant, multiracial society. Although the presentation ultimately fails to convince, in large part because the text's emphasis on racial harmony is undermined by the same class biases that inform Dawood's other works, *Water Under the Bridge* is notable for its celebration of the urban middle and upper class as the source of a newfound racial harmony.

Because it is the locus of so much power, Nairobi is a fortress where barriers are set up, where certain people are excluded, and where the repressive strength of the armed forces lie ready to crush trespassers. In popular and serious works alike, characters are constantly coming up against blocks, dead ends, closed doors, and enforcers of the law—the city is the "closed road to *wapi* [where]" of Wambakha's novel by that title. Text after text show that many apparatuses of colonial Kenya meant to enforce divisions along racial lines have been maintained and, in some cases, even strengthened in postcolonial Kenya. For instance, a common theme for Kikuyu writers—one laid out by Ngugi already in *A Grain of Wheat* (1966)—is the derailment of land resettlement schemes by corrupt politicians. Workers who form cooperatives to buy white-owned ranches after independence are regularly outmaneuvered by the city-based politicians and business owners in stories like Sam Githinji's *Struggling for Survival* (1983), Maura Waweru's *The Siege* (1985), or Ngugi's *Petals of Blood* (1977).

From the *askaris* in the security industry through the police, army, and prison system, the literature shows that postcolonial Kenya is dominated by armed force. Ironically, in the security industry it is often the poorest classes who take jobs as *askaris* and are charged with the task of protecting the property of the wealthy. In *The Siege*, for example, Kairu is forced to take a job with Paka Guards, but is fired for reading too much and attempting to organize his underpaid and exploited co-workers. If a relatively resourceful character like Kairu is powerless against these forces, the "lonely boys" and other marginal characters have even less recourse. Meja and Maina in Mwangi's *Kill Me Quick* (1973) or Eddy Chura in Thomas Akare's *The Slums* (1981) may amuse the reader with their antics, but in the end they come up against the harsh reality that they are being shut off from the promises of the city.

What these stories demonstrate is that for many Kenyans the postcolonial city is a fortress where the legal system protects property first and foremost. The crime story subgenre is particularly rich in this regard, demonstrating time and again the arbitrary and brutal nature of the police force and the prison system. Kamiti Prison is perhaps the most widely written-about landmark in Nairobi: although unmarked on most city maps, it and other penal institutions are key places in both popular fiction from the likes of Mangua and Kiriamiti, as well as more serious works based on the writers' personal experiences. Benjamin Garth Bundeh's *Birds of Kamiti* (1991) and Wahome Mutahi's *The Jail Bugs* (1992), for example, are remarkably similar to the nonfiction exposés by activists like Ngugi and Koigi wa Wamwere, since all these writers have first-hand experience in Kenyan jails. Kamiti, at Nairobi's northeast edge, has particular significance as the site where

Dedan Kimathi, the most celebrated of the Mau Mau rebels, died. For writers like Ngugi, therefore, Kamiti is where colonialism and neocolonialism meet, particularly given the fact that no official recognition has been made by the Kenyan government of Kimathi's death there.

In short, a reading of Kenyan novels demonstrates that the city, Nairobi in particular, is where postcolonial society's dynamics are most strongly apparent. Understanding Nairobi's urban geography requires an appreciation of the various contests and conflicts that constitute it. In the following chapters, we will see how these conflicts are presented in the proliferation of popular novels, in the paradigmatic works of Meja Mwangi, and in relation to issues of gender in the city.

Chapter 6

Heartbeats and Afromances: Popular Novels and the City

Voices in the Dark, Kenya's first urban novel, had been in circulation for only a year before the genre's second major landmark—Charles Mangua's *Son of Woman* (1971)—made its appearance. *Son of Woman* was the first unambiguously popular novel from Kenya and is still the most interesting of its type. The contrast with Kibera's work could hardly be greater, however; reading the two in tandem provides a sense of the extremes of Nairobi's portrait in the Kenyan novel. Both novels feature urban settings. However, instead of darkness, depression, and death, *Son of Woman* shows a city of light, adventure, and life. To be sure, Mangua describes the actual poverty, grime, and degradation that constitute life in Nairobi's slums, often in even more graphic detail than Kibera, but the tone of disillusionment, despair, and bitterness that character-ized *Voices in the Dark* gives way in Mangua's story to an attitude of cynical humor and fatalistic opportunism.

It would be hard to find a greater contrast than the one between Kibera's morose intellectual, Gerald Timundu, and Mangua's happy-go-lucky protagonist, Dodge Kiunyu.

Timundu belongs to the tradition of Ngugian characters like Njoroge, Waiyaki, and Mugo—characters who take themselves and their history seriously and who grow disillusioned when their dreams are betrayed or unfulfilled. Kiunyu, conversely, is a totally new type of character in Kenyan literature: the romantic and celebrated outlaw—a stock character, it should be noted, in the American popular fiction from which Kenyan popular writing draws much of its inspiration. Both Timundu and Kiunyu attended university, and both are dissatisfied with the dead-end, white-collar careers for which they qualify. Where Timundu intellectualizes his situation, however, Kiunyu is a man of action. When Timundu confronts injustice and inequality, he writes an esoteric play about it, while Kiunyu's response is to make sure he gets the biggest possible piece of an unjustly divided pie, by whatever means necessary. Kiunyu is not the type of outlaw to be found in Mau Mau novels, where a rebel, however flawed, is nonetheless fighting for a greater, communal cause. Rather, he is an individualist who flouts the law for purely selfish reasons.

Given his deprived childhood, Kiunyu might have turned into a version of the "lonely boy" whom Kibera pictured standing outside the storefronts looking hungrily in—except that Kiunyu presents himself as quickly hardened to the realities of street life. This is no sensitive child, but a wily and street-hardened maverick. Kiunyu's narration is alternately abusive and conspiratorial towards the reader, but always defiant. Despite the title, Dodge Kiunyu is connected and obligated to no one:

> I am the son of woman and I'll repeat it till your elephant ears ache. Never had a dad in my blinking life. My whoring ma could never figure out who my pop was. A very short memory—that's what she had. It was one of the scores of men who took her for a bedride but she wasn't bothered to remember who among them I resembled. That's my mother. (7)

Dodge Kiunyu is an urban orphan whose mother, an Eastleigh prostitute, dies while Kiunyu is still young. Although he eventually manages to attend university and land a civil service job (ironically, in the Ministry of Labor and Social Services), Kiunyu's career is littered with illicit dealings and fast living, climaxing with a bungled robbery. He is arrested for fighting in a Nanyuki bar and would have been caught with stolen money except that Tonia, a prostitute and childhood friend, had previously taken it from him. After a year in prison, Kiunyu marries Tonia, and they move to an oceanside cottage in Mombasa, recognizing that theirs is a marriage of convenience, but that both are ready to settle down and reform their lives.

The action in *Son of Woman* is distinctly urban, beginning in the Nairobi slums and moving to Nakuru, then to Nanyuki, and finally to Mombasa. The city in Mangua's text is a playground, albeit a dangerous one. The rootlessness and alienation that form the source of impotence and dysfunction in *Voices in the Dark* are translated into opportunity in *Son of Woman*. To be sure, Nairobi's underbelly is presented, even emphasized:

> We are staring at a row of shanty houses in front of us. I am wondering why we must always have dust and flies. Dust and flies, smoke and evil smells, that's what we've got. Nude hungry children and dirty whoring mothers—that is the order of the day. This is Eastleigh. Most famous place in Nairobi for advanced prostitution. (26)

By the same token, however, the first thing Kiunyu notices on a brief visit to the village is its unpleasant smell and how boring and dingy it is: "The stench is the opposite of that normally exuded by prostitutes. It is the smell of sweat and filthy armpits added to rotten bananas, snuff, onions" (39). The village of Kaheti itself is dark and "ghostly" (40). Nostalgia for an idyllic, rural life has no place in *Son of Woman*; Kiunyu's orientation is to the present and the future.

Kiunyu, up front about his vices and shortcomings, is an ultimately likeable character. He has the habit of freely addressing the reader, suggesting that he is in fact only doing what all of us wish we could do, particularly in the way he reacts to authority (police or bosses) and in the way he follows his instinctive greed. We follow Kiunyu's story with amusement and bemusement, and always with a nagging question (posed by the narrator himself) lurking in the back of our mind: Can we really trust anything he says? Kiunyu's "conversion" in the end is particularly suspicious. Mangua has created a sarcastic, cynical, and happy-go-lucky character whose concluding claim that he is "not interested" in any more illegal gain is highly suspect:

> So there you are. You know all about me. Like mother like son. My mother was a whore and I am getting married to a whore . . . . I'll write some poems for Tonia too and try to get them published. If you know any other easy ways to keep the dough flowing in, send your ideas to me. Just drop me a line. You can bet your bottom dollar I'll be needing them. But nothing that will land me in jail. No sir, I'm not interested. (159)

Beyond the fast-moving and irreverent plot, the novel succeeds because this ending is so obviously parodic. Kiunyu's final repentance, in the "conversion" tradition found in so many other Kenyan popular novels, is transparently unconvincing. Any reader knows that Kiunyu's interest in "other easy ways" to make money will inevitably lead to more adventures, and no one could have been surprised at the appearance of Mangua's equally action-packed sequel, *Son of Woman in Mombasa* (1986).

Son of Woman became the archetype for a style of writing that has since come to dominate the Kenyan literary scene. A significant majority of the novels published in Kenya since 1970 might be categorized as popular, and include a wide variety of adventures, romances, crime and detective stories. Perhaps because it has become so dominant, popular writing has provoked one of the most heated critical debates in East African literature over the past two decades. These types of texts, typically characterized by shallow characters, simple plots, and an emphasis on action rather than contemplation, are generally acknowledged to be potboilers, with an eye to turning a profit rather than contributing to Kenya's literary culture. Many of them (including *Son of Woman*) were created for novel-writing competitions sponsored by publishing firms. Popular Western authors, most notably James Hadley Chase, Agatha Christie, Ian Fleming, and Robert Ludlum, are frequently cited as models for this genre, as are popular Hollywood films.

Critics both locally and internationally have vilified the turn toward popular writing in Kenya, condemning these works as amoral, pornographic, lacking a serious message, and generally being a bad influence on Kenyan youth. Chris Wanjala, one of Kenya's most prolific critics, has been among the most outspoken in this regard. Seven years after the appearance of the much-imitated *Son of Woman*, he would write:

> There is a case of literature in Kenya which is a trashy and scabrous imitation of brothel and low life, especially yarned for the low-brow reader in this country. It portrays the depraved scenes of sex, the dilemma of the prostitute and the cancer of unemployment.
> (*The Season of Harvest*, 135-6)

It could not have been simply the portrayal of these depravities that disturbed Wanjala and others, since prostitution and unemployment might just as easily form the subject of the socially committed literature that has also been significant in East African writing. Rather, it is popular fiction's sensational and uncritical celebration of these blights of modernity that makes it morally reprobate. The individualistic outlaw who is the *sine qua non* of the popular genre is not, by these lights, an appropriate social model.

In the Preface to C. Okello's *The Prophet* (1978), Wanjala quotes the manager of Uzima Press, Reverend Horace Etemesi, as saying that the church-run publishing house wants to maintain the "moral tone of society and indeed the dignity of literature" by avoiding "maimed" and "diseased" portrayals of "*rag-bag* characters in *rag-bag* language" (ii). In a similar vein, and in the same year, the writer Asenath Bole Odaga suggested in a presentation at Nairobi's Institute of African Studies that

> this sort of literature is serving little or no good purpose, since it is mostly on sex, and tends to have as its heroes men and women who are actually anti-progress, mediocre, who lack imagination, ideals, initiative and positive goals in life. ("Popular Literature in East Africa," 16)

Taking up Taban lo Liyong's famous 1960s-era metaphor of East Africa as a literary wasteland in need of watering, the pioneering critic Bernth Lindfors commented in the 1970s that "the literary desert, after a slow and tentative initial flowering, is now germinating its first full harvest of weeds" (*Popular Literatures in Africa*, 58).

If Mangua started the popular trend, David Maillu established it beyond any doubt. Maillu is among the most productive, innovative, and controversial of contemporary Kenyan writers, with over forty published books of various types, and the sheer variety of his work makes it difficult to characterize as a whole. As Lindfors suggests, there are many Maillus at work: "Maillu the moralist, Maillu the practical psychologist, Maillu the homespun philosopher, Maillu the comedian, Maillu the popular publisher" (*Popular Literatures in Africa*, 97). Thematically, most of Maillu's works explore the complex issue of what it means to be African in a twentieth-century urban setting. Formally, his narratives stretched the limits of received literary categories, thanks to Maillu's willingness to experiment. Whatever one thinks of his work (and his critics are numerous), Maillu must be credited with being among the most persistent, unpredictable and creative East African writers today.

Although he has also written children's stories and nonfiction treatises on religion and philosophy, Maillu is best known as the author and self-publisher of popular best sellers. Early in his writing career, Maillu made a survey of potential readers in order to discover their interests. Respondents highlighted half a dozen topics—politics, sex, human relations, religion, death, and money—and Maillu tailored his writing accordingly, quickly producing best sellers with titles that speak for themselves: *Unfit for Human Consumption* (1973), *My Dear Bottle* (1973), *After 4:30* (1974; about what happens between bosses and secretaries after working hours), *Trouble* (1974), *No!* (1976) and *PO Box I Love You, Via My Heart* (1991), among others. The works he wrote during the 1970s in particular established Maillu's reputation as Kenya's leading popular writer. His overt presentation of sex, without any redeeming moral lessons, led to his excoriation by the local critical establishment, and for a time his books were banned in Tanzania. In recent years, however, criticism of Maillu's work has given way to a grudging respect, in part because of his sheer longevity and in part because of his willingness to be innovative. Lindfors, formerly a vocal critic of Maillu's work, has of late revised his previous assessment and suggests that in the 1990s there appeared a "new David Maillu," thanks in large measure to his more recent moralistic novels that contain explicitly didactic messages (*Popular Literatures in Africa*, 87-100).

Despite their superficial differences, however, Maillu's popular writing and his more recent moralistic works are remarkably similar. Both are driven by urban rather than rural dynamics. Both treat the rural setting in a one-dimensional manner: as a haven from and antithesis of the city. Both, despite Maillu's reputation for writing immoral prose, end up presenting a "lesson" to the reader. Above all, both are obsessed by the topic of gender roles in contemporary Kenyan society.

After 4:30, Maillu's best-known work, is typical of his popular best sellers. Originally published in 1974 and revised in a second edition in 1987, it is the text that established Maillu's reputation for racy prose. Stories of schoolgirls reading the novel under their desks have been commonplace ever since the book has been in print. *After 4:30* is organized around a series of testimonials, presented in the free verse style popularized by Okot p'Bitek, which is acclaimed on the cover of the revised 1987 edition (quoted below) as the "new poetic style that is quite popular in Africa." The first testimony comes from Emili Katango, whose surname invokes the idea of loitering or idle wandering. Emili is a secretary in a government office in Nairobi, and her opening statement makes clear the general direction of the narrative:

> Call me Emili Katango
> that's me
> the gate into my kingdom
> opens wide
> men don't like me
> they say I'm loose.
> I look for a doctor
> to tighten me.
> Somehow. (1)

We also hear from other urban voices: Lili, a slightly older and more experienced secretary who nevertheless has all manner of difficulties fending off the sexual advances of her boss; the prostitute, Susi; Lili's boyfriend, Daniel; and Mwelu, Emili's younger sister. The various speakers present a loose collage of experiences that results in an urban portrait of desolation, broken relationships, prostitution, exploitation, and violence. In the end, as with many other popular works, Emili the prostitute is in fact a cipher for the city: Nairobi is the whore who destroys traditional male-female roles and time-honored family structures.

After 4:30, despite the indignant, moralistic outcry against it, is profoundly didactic. It titillates, but ultimately returns the readers to their world with a basically conservative conclusion. At the story's close, Emili is nursing her son, who is her main hope and the reason she clings to life despite its disappointments. The message is clear: Salvation for the city/prostitute is through finding a male protector and a return to traditional male authority. Emili concludes:

> Child, dear son
> I bank on you. Stand up
> my shield. Your loving Mother
> is proud of you
> you are other men
> in many, many ways.
> In you
> my husband and my father return. (248)

Maillu's popular novels proved so successful that he was able to establish his own publishing enterprise, Comb Books, later bogged down by legal and financial problems and replaced by Maillu Publishing House. While it lasted, Comb Books produced titles from Maillu and other writers, all in the same popular mode as *After 4:30*. Jasinta Mote's *The Flesh* (1975), for example, claims to be the first-person account of a real-life Nairobi prostitute, "produced" with some help by David Maillu. Maillu's market research, clearly, had paid off.

In the 1970s, Kenyan publishing houses, well aware of the success of Mangua and Maillu, initiated special series to accommodate popular texts. Heinemann (later East African Educational Publishers) was first with its Spear Book series, followed shortly thereafter by Afromances from Transafrica, Pacesetters from Macmillan, and Heartbeat Books from East African Publishing House. While Longman (later Longhorn) did not set up a special category, its Masterpiece Series includes many titles that fit the category of popular writing. In addition to their titillating content, these texts tend to be short (around 100 pages), featuring colorful pictures on the cover and enticing titles such as *Love and Learn* (Mary Kize, 1974), *Fire and Vengeance* (J. C. Onyango-Abuje, 1975), *Lover in the Sky* (Sam Kahiga, 1975), or *A Girl Cannot Go on Laughing All the Time* (Magaga Alot, 1975). John Nottingham reported in an interview with Bernth Lindfors that Transafrica Publishers at one point hired a Ugandan writer to produce as many such texts as he could, with the plan to publish them under a variety of pseudonyms (*Mazungumzo: Interviews with East African Writers, Publishers, Editors and Scholars*, 120). The most prolific of the popular lines has been EAEP's Spear Books, whose first title is a classic: Rosemary Owino's *Sugar Daddy's Lover* (1975) is about the seduction of a schoolgirl by a wealthy Nairobi businessman. The twenty years following *Sugar Daddy's Lover* saw the addition of 35 more titles to the Spear Book series.

Two major plot lines dominate Kenya's popular novels: the "my life in crime" story, usually narrated from a male's perspective; and the "prostitute's tale," from a female's. (Mangua's *Son of Woman*, not surprisingly, managed to include both plot lines with the intertwined stories of Dodge and Tonia.) Classics of the "my life in crime" group include the immensely popular *My Life in Crime* (Kiriamiti, 1984), *Shortcut to Hell* (Kitololo, 1983), *A Brief Assignment* (Ndii, 1976), *The Mystery Smugglers* (Ruheni, 1975) and *The Bhang Syndicate* (Saisi, 1984), among others. The story line typically follows the adventures of gangsters and thugs, both in and out of prison, usually with a moralistic ending that unconvincingly emphasizes the depravity and emptiness of all that has gone before. The "prostitute's tale," meanwhile, typically follows a woman's descent into lurid living, only to conclude with a moralistic change of heart or the death of the protagonist. Maillu's *After 4:30* is comprised of such a tale, as are *Sugar Daddy's Lover* (Owino), *Whispers* (Muli wa Kyendo), and *Twilight Woman* (Akare).

While these texts are modeled on Western popular stories and films, most lend a specifically Kenyan flavor or twist to the narrative. In many cases, the stories refer to significant events from recent Kenyan history: Geteria's *Nice People* (1992), inspired in part by an article on AIDS by *Washington Post* reporter Blaine Harden, addresses corruption in the medical establishment and AIDS in Nairobi; *Black Gold of Chepkube* (Geteria's first novel, 1985), deals with a scheme to smuggle coffee from Uganda during the coffee "boom" of the mid-1970s; *Life and Times of a Bank Robber* (1988) is Kaggia Kimani's first-person account of a spectacular bank robbery in Nakuru in 1970; Mwangi's *The Bushtrackers* (1979) follows poachers in Kenyan game parks. These stories tend to feature classic Nairobi characters like the sugar daddy and the street urchin, or they are based on urban legends built around real-life figures like the legendary Nairobi police detective, Patrick Shaw. (At times the resemblance of these dramatic stories to real-life events is coincidental but eerie. A highly publicized manhunt for a criminal known as Wanugu, which ended in a deadly shootout with the Kenyan police in Nakuru in mid-1996, has uncanny similarities to Mangua's story about Dodge Kiunyu—published 25 years earlier!)

Frequently, popular novels will emphasize the opulence and decadence of the lives of the rich and famous. If the stories go into what might be considered excessive detail about Kenya's hotels, lodges, game parks, and resorts, or if they spend an inordinate amount of time detailing the fancy cars and dress of the wealthy, it should be remembered that they are in fact providing a window on a world to which most Kenyans do not have access. Kahiga, for example, features an elaborate description of a fancy house in a wealthy Nairobi suburb in *Lover in the Sky* (1975); Maillu depicts Maasai Mara game park and Keekorok Lodge in *Operation DXT* (1986); and Duchi emphasizes the details of Nairobi's Hotel Boulevard, Amboseli game park and other tourists sites in *Assassins on Safari* (1983).

Sometimes a story will be directly allegorical, and in this respect popular fiction (thanks to its pose as an improbable tale in a far-off place) is able to present a strong critique of Kenyan society. In Karanja wa Kang'ethe's *Mission to Gehenna*, for example, Kimuri and Keega are mysteriously transported to Gehenna, the kingdom of Satan Lucifer, where we encounter a rather familiar world. Satan is dictator in a land where cheating, corruption, and killing are commonplace; politicians are greedy, slums abound; religion is corrupt; and there are epidemic diseases (including AIDS) and employment problems. In short, the central village of *Ahera* (Hades) bears more than a passing resemblance to Nairobi.

On the other hand, a large number of these stories are unambiguously set outside of Kenya, presenting a protagonist's experiences in Europe or in North America. Maillu's *PO Box I Love You, Via My Heart* (1991) is set in Sweden, Mwangi's *The Return of Shaka* (1989) in the U.S., and Mak'Oloo's *Times Beyond* (1991) in Hungary. Alternatively, they might present a story set either in a generic African setting, address a social problem specific to some other part of Africa, or focus on colonial issues. Maillu's adventure hero Benni Kamba ("Agent 009") saves the continent from dictators who are superpower puppets in *The Equatorial Assignment* (1980) and from a deadly AIDS-like virus in *Operation DXT* (1986). South African apartheid is the target of Mwangi's *Bread of Sorrow* (1987) and of Ng'weno's *The Men from Pretoria* (1975). Gicheru's *The Mixers* (1991) treats interracial marriage in the Kenyan colonial setting. Even when they focus on a non-Kenyan setting or on colonial issues that belong to an era well in the past, however, Kenyan writers may be creating allegories of the situation in which they live.

Despite the criticism from various quarters, these texts have proven immensely popular in Kenya since their first appearance in the 1970s, and they have affected the way "serious" texts are written as well. Ngugi's first post-1970 novel, *Petals of Blood* (1977), was clearly influenced by the new fad for detective stories; it opens as a murder mystery, and while it quickly becomes much more than that, it is clear that Ngugi was responding to the newly popular mystery genre. Similarly, Ndissio-Otieno's *A Blurring Horizon* (1991) is on the surface a murder mystery in the popular style, while in fact presenting an outstandingly lyrical analysis of the pressures on first-generation Kenyan entrepreneurs. Marjorie Oludhe Macgoye's *Murder in Majengo* (1972) also sets itself up as a detective story, but turns out to be a remarkable exploration of the urban Luo community in postcolonial Kenya.

Nonetheless, there is a clear stigma attached to popular writing in Kenya today. Writers tend to be labelled as either "popular" or "serious" writers, which can be particularly problematic for those who manage to operate in both registers. One of the main dilemmas for Meja Mwangi, for example, has been the difficulty of maintaining credibility with the critics after writing a number of popular thrillers during the late 1970s and 1980s. David Maillu is another writer who has written texts belonging to both "popular" and "serious" categories. Although the brothers Sam Kahiga and Leonard Kibera collaborated on a collection of short stories, Kibera is remembered primarily as the "serious" author of *Voices in the Dark*, while Kahiga has produced a number of fast-paced popular novels with catchy titles like *The Girl from Abroad* (1974), *Lover in the Sky* (1975), and *Paradise Farm* (1993).

Can popular literature be taken seriously? After all, these are stories that rely on formulas, clichés, and stereotypes, where suspense and shock are more important than originality or depth of thought, their explicit purpose being entertainment rather than the exploration of ideas. Popular novels are intended for a mass audience that has no special training or education; they belong to the bottom half of a dialectic, pitting "high" or "elite" forms of expression against "low" or "common" forms. Above all, if you are concerned with the moral impact of stories, this assortment of "rag-bag characters in rag-bag language" seems hardly worthy of thoughtful attention.

To make matters worse, many of Kenya's popular novels reinscribe and reinforce many of the stereotypes and tropes of the Western models on which they are based. They mimic many of the same generalities and essentialisms about African "primitivism" that are found in Western examples. Sometimes the portrayal is negative, suggesting that traditional African society is a primitive backwater whose inhabitants are lazy, uneducated, and superstitious, as in Pat Ngurukie's *I Will Be Your Substitute* (1984) or Yusuf Dawood's works. Sometimes, going to the other extreme, traditional life is so romanticized as to appear Utopian, as in Maillu's *The Ayah* (1986). Occasionally, as in Mwangi Ruheni's *The Minister's Daughter* (1975), a novel will manage to present both ideas simultaneously.

While critics charge that Kenya's popular writing is both symptom and catalyst of disillusionment, moral decay and social decadence, its defenders point out that since this is clearly what people choose to read (hence the label), popular fiction fulfills the dual function of entertaining and cultivating reading habits. Furthermore, proponents add that popular writing can be particularly effective in highlighting genuine social dilemmas in the process of telling what is essentially an escapist tale. Popular literature is by this account "the true mirror of the hidden reality of the region's social experiences" (Francis Imbuga, "East African Literature in the 1980s," *Matatu* 10, 1993, 127).

If we accept the notion, put forth most elegantly by the American critic Fredric Jameson, that cultural and artistic forms of expression, in addition to whatever else they do, present responses to a society's contradictions on a metaphorical or symbolic level, then we can see how popular literature can, often unwittingly, contribute to the "serious" task of understanding society. Narrative, according to Jameson, represents an ideological and aesthetic manifestation of broader social dynamics. Literature, including popular literature, contains a "political unconscious" that may be read as a "symbolic meditation on the destiny of community" (*The Political Unconscious: Narrative as a Socially Symbolic Act*, 70). Novelists, in other words, may be showing us about the history, sociology, and politics of a place even when they are simply pretending to present an entertaining story. In short, we can read between the lines to discover what a novel is telling us about the "hidden reality" of a time and place.

It is precisely for this reason that reading Kenyan novels can provide insights into the obsessions and fears connected with urbanization, which is itself a symbol for the general social tensions and problems of Kenya today. Since novels contain a "political unconscious" that is an attempt to resolve society's contradictions, and since the fundamental contradictions in Kenyan society are at their strongest in the city, it is no surprise that here is where so many works—serious as well as popular—find their content. Popular novels may be the most fertile territory of all because of their disingenuous claims to be pure entertainments.

What, then, can be discovered in the "political unconscious" of Kenyan popular novels? What is the "hidden reality" they reveal? In general, to use the Kenyan critic Abdul Jan Mohammed's terminology (from *Manichean Aesthetics: The Politics of Literature in Colonial Africa*), we can lump texts into one of two categories, depending on whether they are guided by hegemonic or counter-hegemonic impulses— that is, whether they support the political and social *status quo* or whether they bring it into question. Hegemonic texts reinforce and justify the existing political order and dominant cultural mores. Counterhegemonic texts challenge them.

Most popular works are, at least on the surface, guided by hegemonic impulses, which would make sense since a critique of the social order is likely to present itself in as serious and respectable a form as possible. Counterhegemonic works, therefore, tend to present themselves as more "serious" disillusionment novels or novels of political critique. There are, however, at least a few openly counterhegemonic popular works, and because they appear in the guise of popular fiction, they can contain a critique that would be censored as a matter of course in a different forum. Wahome Mutahi's *The Jail Bugs* (1992), for instance, features a colorful cover and a breezy, humorous narrative voice reminiscent of other popular tales of crime and prison life. The blurb on the cover emphasizes the "humorous style that has established Wahome Mutahi as Kenya's leading satirist." Despite this posture as yet another comic account in the "my life in crime" genre, however, the novel contains a blistering critique of Kenya's penal system and the breakdown of justice in the country that would be crystal clear to any Kenyan reader. It is especially gripping when we realize that Mutahi himself spent fifteen months in a Kenyan prison. Kang'ethe's *Mission to Gehenna*, mentioned above, is equally critical although less direct in its allusion to specifically Kenyan events and places.

These few exceptions aside, Kenyan popular fiction most often contains a conservative, hegemonic message. Frequently it is a law and order message: that a life of crime, despite its excitement and adventure, in the end will not pay. Most of the "my life in crime" stories feature an ending similar to that in *Son of Woman*, in which the narrator repents and vows to live on the right side of the law. In *Life and Times of a Bank Robber* (1988), Kimani's narrator, John Penny, completes his prison term to be reunited with his brother, his ailing mother, and the nuns who were nursing her. He attributes his release from "the drug called a criminal mind" not to the prison system itself but to an examination of conscience: "I saw former associates in crime die poor and in disgraceful circumstances in prison and got more and more convinced that crime does not pay" (132). The less reflective *My Life in Crime* (1989), from John Kiriamiti, concludes with a similar vow:

> I am a reformed person. I am wholly decided to be on
> the right side of the law for as long as I live. The main
> reason is that I have learnt that crime does not pay.
> Another reason is that I have now learnt a lot of skills—
> signwriting, silkscreen printing and the art of paint-
> ing—that I did not know before and I would never
> have got a chance to know. (215)

Such testimonies serve to support the legitimacy of the existing order and existing authority. The jacket cover to Frank
Saisi's *The Bhang Syndicate* (1984), in which a police inspector helps to break up an international drug-trafficking cartel,
notes that Kip "feels morally committed to the triumph of the
forces of Kenya law." The Preface to Daniel Ng'ang'a's *Young
Today, Old Tomorrow* (1971), a moralistic tale in which a returned World War II veteran seeks revenge on his brother-in-
law, was written by then Vice President Daniel arap Moi, who
praised Kenya's fiction writers and particularly those who
demonstrate how "the long arm of the law remains active at
all times."

A related hegemonic message is that bad people will ultimately be punished for their deeds, while those with good
intentions, despite moments of adversity, will be rewarded in
the end. This is particularly true in romances like Pat
Ngurukie's *Tough Choices* (1991), in which Florence
Mwangi's children oppose her remarriage, only to drop their
objections in the end. As we will see in Chapter Eight of this
text, much of the popular literature contains an especially conservative, hegemonic message when it comes to gender roles,
supporting male authority in traditional and modern relationships alike. In *Tough Choices*, things turn out right for Florence Mwangi because her new husband, Stanley, is finally
installed "as head of the family," where "he played his role
perfectly" (101).

The problem for hegemonic texts—and the point at which
they become interesting—arises when they present conflicts
and dilemmas that they can only paper over in an inadequate,

superficial and unsustainable manner. While they try desperately to resolve conflicts in a manner that reinforces established norms, they ultimately fail. Their failure is evinced most clearly in their endings. In order to create a hegemonic message, in order to support the *status quo* and to resolve what are in fact unresolvable problems, these narratives resort to outrageous, impossible, and incredible conclusions. The rapid about-face of the children in *Tough Choices*, for instance, is only remotely believable because their characters remained shallow throughout the story. The triumph of law and order over chaos, as it appears in novels like *The Bhang Syndicate*, relies on luck and machinations that ring false. The penitent conclusions of all the "my life in crime" works seem equally hollow.

Almost all popular novels rely on these contrived endings. In his study of Meja Mwangi's *Striving for the Wind*, for example, the Swedish critic Lars Johansson has noted that the character of the exploitative landowner Baba Pesa "is considerably inverted towards the end of the novel, but his inversion is not developed in a way to make it convincing" (*In the Shadow of Neocolonialism: Meja Mwangi's Novels 1973-1990*, 123). Unjust land distribution, which is the underlying problem, remains intact, and Baba Pesa's resolution to be more humane strikes one as an inadequate, short-term fix. Similarly, in Sam Kahiga's *Paradise Farm* (1993), Joe and Janet lead exciting and self-indulgent lives of travel, drugs, and sexual exploits, beginning in Kenya and leading on to New York City and back to Kenya. At the novel's close, they suddenly begin to think about the welfare of the workers on their farm. Their change of heart, like Baba Pesa's, comes as an unconvincing afterthought:

> Build them good houses. Build their children a school there on the farm. Double their salaries. We'll think of something. It will be *their* paradise too. (300)

Far more successful, by contrast, are those texts that either do not attempt to force plot closure or those that do it in an obviously parodic way, which is why we end up where we began: with Charles Mangua's *Son of Woman*. One of the reasons that this remains the most interesting of Kenya's popular novels, in addition to being the first, is because it leaves the story open-ended. To be sure, there is a gesture toward a hegemonic, law-and-order conclusion, but it is so weak and half-hearted as to be pure parody.

Popular novels, almost all of which are obsessed with urban characters and conflicts, have completely changed the face of Kenyan literature since their first appearance in 1970, and they seem likely to continue dominating the Kenyan literary scene for the foreseeable future. Their value for the student of Kenyan literature, beyond serving as examples of escapist entertainment, lies in their often disingenuous portrayal of Nairobi's social contradictions—despite their attempts to suppress them. In the next chapter, we turn to the works of Meja Mwangi, a writer with an exceptional flair for creating popular stories. Mwangi's writing covers the gamut of styles and themes found in the Kenyan novel, including but also moving beyond popular texts, and as such makes an excellent case study for the various representations and roles of the urban landscape in the Kenyan novel.

Chapter 7

Tracking the "Tramp of the Damned": The Novels of Meja Mwangi

Already in the middle 1970s, Meja Mwangi was being feted as "the next Ngugi wa Thiong'o" of Kenyan writing. When he burst onto the scene with the award-winning picaresque novel *Kill Me Quick* (1973), Mwangi was hailed in various quarters as a rising star in the East African literary constellation who was helping to disprove Taban lo Liyong's oft-cited claim that East Africa was a literary desert. Since then, Meja Mwangi has gone on to establish himself as one of the most prolific of Kenyan writers, publishing 11 novels in 17 years in addition to short stories, children's books, and working on a variety of film projects. He is the recipient of numerous awards, in Kenya and abroad, and his works have been translated into six languages; two of his novels have been made into films.

If there is a single writer whose work is representative of the entire range of Kenyan narrative fiction today, it is Meja Mwangi. In his writings we find the full range of thematic concerns that run through Kenyan writing as a whole; we also are faced once again with the tensions between popular and serious writing that have so occupied Kenyan critics. Most importantly, from our point of view, Mwangi was the first Kenyan novelist to seize on and fully develop the urban dynamics that were first explored in Leonard Kibera's *Voices in the Dark*.

One might divide Mwangi's work into three major categories. The first category comprises his Mau Mau novels. The armed resistance to British colonialism in Kenya, which came to be known as the Mau Mau revolt and reached its height in the 1950s, was a formative experience for many Kenyans, especially for those from the Kikuyu ethnic group to which Mwangi belongs. Like other Kikuyu writers—Ngugi, Mangua, Wachira, Gicheru, Kahiga, Karoki, Waciuma and others—Mwangi found material for his early novels in the Mau Mau experience, resulting in *Carcase for Hounds* (1974) and *Taste of Death* (1975).

The thrillers that Mwangi began to produce in the late 1970s and 1980s—beginning with *The Bushtrackers* (1979)—form a second category of texts that has put him at the heart of the raging critical debate in the Kenyan literary establishment over the merits of popular literature. As a result, Mwangi finds himself in a position similar to that of David Maillu: although he has produced a variety of works, the pejorative label of "popular writer" has tainted his reputation in the academic establishment.

The third category of Mwangian writing consists of his city novels. Mwangi's urban trilogy—*Kill Me Quick* (1973), *Going Down River Road* (1976), and *The Cockroach Dance* (1979)—is compelling and innovative in its treatment of what is arguably the most pressing contemporary social problem in Kenya: the effects of the rapid urbanization that the country has experienced since independence in 1963. It is fair to say that critical acclaim for Mwangi as a writer has come predominantly from these tales of city life.

Because of the variety of texts that Mwangi has produced, it can be difficult to define his narrative succinctly. Most observers tend to either focus on one of his categories of writing (the Mau Mau books, the thrillers, or the urban tales) or to contrast the superficiality of the thrillers with the more successful city novels. Conventional wisdom has it that Mwangi's serious, urban novels have been compromised by his popular works, and that this rising star, this "new Ngugi," has not shone as brightly as originally promised. However, such an assessment glosses Mwangi's works in a superficial manner; the situation appears more complex if we view his work as a whole.

The first full-length study of Mwangi's work, Lars Johansson's *In the Shadow of Neocolonialism: A Study of Meja Mwangi's Novels, 1973-1990* (1992), argues that Mwangi's novels display ideological ambiguities for two reasons. In the first place they are affected by what the Russian formalist Bakhtin calls an external, "authoritative discourse" as well as a personal, "internally-persuasive discourse." The struggle between these opposed discourses results in the sometimes conflicting voices in Mwangi's narrative (4-5). In the second place, Johansson uses a model offered by the Marxist critic Fredric Jameson to assert that Mwangi's novels are affected by crucial social contradictions that form their "political unconscious" (6). The concepts of contesting discourses and of a political unconscious allow us to understand the otherwise surprising incongruities in Mwangi's writing.

In Johansson's view, the basic social contradiction in Kenyan society is the issue of land and land distribution:

> This issue was not at all concluded at Independence, as we will see, and is the "event" of recent Kenyan political history which I hypothesize as constituting the "social basis of the text." (7)

Johansson consequently sees the social injustices of neocolonialism as the driving dynamic in Mwangi's stories. Mwangi's urban novels, he suggests, are the most interesting because they display competing discourses that result from social forces; they are thus multidimensional. His thrillers, because they are generally put in non-Kenyan or even non-African settings, are consequently removed from the "real relations" in Kenyan society; their unidimensional nature results from their foreign settings and their foreign characters.

While Johansson offers an excellent overall model for conceptualizing Mwangi's work, his emphasis on land issues alone represents an incomplete view of the "real relations" of contemporary Kenyan society. Land tenure and land alienation are certainly among the most important social issues in postindependence Kenya, but as our readings of other texts have shown, they must be seen in light of the broader social picture. Johansson is at base interested in the origin and content of the ideology of Mwangi's work; to understand these fully we need to look at the broader tradition-modernity conflicts that are manifested in Mwangi's narrative.

As an examination of his various texts will show, Mwangi's Mau Mau novels and his thrillers portray these conflicts in fairly conventional ways. It is in his urban novels where Mwangi has made his most original and perhaps most lasting contributions to Kenyan writing. His vivid portrayals of Nairobi's marginal spaces and the people who inhabit them cut to the core of postcolonial Kenyan social reality, showing the city to be the crucial locus of social tensions.

The city also plays a key role in Mwangi's personal history. Around 1970, he moved to Nairobi to continue his education. After completing his "O" level exams at Nanyuki secondary school and his "A" level training at Kenyatta College near Nairobi, he applied for but failed to gain admission to the journalism and television broadcasting programs at the University of Nairobi and instead embarked on a career of practical experience with the film industry. Mwangi worked and traveled throughout East Africa as a soundman with the French Broadcasting Corporation (ORTF), and he later joined the staff at the British Council in Nairobi as a film librarian. It was while working for the British Council that he wrote his first novel (although it was the second to be published), *Carcase for Hounds.*

The influence of film on Mwangi's writing cannot be over-emphasized. As a child in Nanyuki, he regularly attended the open-air films offered by the mobile movie theaters that came through town, showing mostly Hollywood productions. After he moved to Nairobi in 1970, Mwangi had a chance to see American and British films on a regular basis. Later, his connections with French television and with the British Council led to jobs on a number of major films that were shot in Kenya. Mwangi was location manager for *Shadow on the Sun* (1988), casting director for *The Kitchen Toto* (1987), and assistant director for the Hollywood hits *Out of Africa* (1985), *Gorillas in the Mist* (1988), and *White Mischief* (1988). Subsequently, he developed a decidedly cinematic vision in his writing, along with a narrative style reminiscent of fast-moving popular film. Mwangi's characters, like many Kenyans of Mwangi's generation and younger, are conversant in tough-guy American slang; they reflect the alienation and individualism most obvious in postcolonial urban Kenya. Not surprisingly, two of Mwangi's novels have been associated with films: *Carcase for Hounds* was made into *Cry Freedom*, and *The Bushtrackers*, which originated as a screenplay collaboration with the North American journalist Gary Strieker, was published to coincide with the film's release.

Although *Carcase for Hounds* was the first novel Mwangi wrote, it was the second to be published and the second of his works to be filmed. It has much in common with Mwangi's other novel about Mau Mau, *Taste of Death*. Both feature the typical Mwangian fast-paced action and snappy dialogue. Each uses an omniscient narrator who presents the perspective of both the Mau Mau fighters and the white government forces opposing them. Both personalize the conflict by setting up an individual Mau Mau leader against an opposing colonial military commander. The film version of *Carcase for*

Hounds, a Nigerian production directed by Ola Balogun under the title *Cry Freedom*, is a fairly loose adaption of Mwangi's original story. The setting is generically African, not specific to Kenya, and Balogun added romantic entanglements not found in Mwangi's original.

Reflections by historians and fiction writers on the effects of Mau Mau and the accompanying state of emergency—so divisive for Kenya as both a colony and a republic—led to debates over historical accuracy versus revisionism. Colonial writers like Robert Ruark and Elspeth Huxley portrayed the Land and Freedom Army atavistically—that is, they saw it as an unfortunate throwback to a savage past—and some Kenyan writers, including Mwangi, have been accused of unwittingly accepting and perpetuating that negative image. Because the national bourgeoisie and the political elite that emerged after independence are not the same people who fought the Mau Mau wars, the argument goes, that history had to be rewritten to downplay the heroism of the guerrilla fighters and to emphasize instead the role of Jomo Kenyatta and other postindependence political leaders. Thus, according to David Maughan-Brown, Mwangi, like Charles Mangua in *A Tail in the Mouth* (1972) and Godwin Wachira in *Ordeal in the Forest* (1968), participates in "criminalizing" the movement through his representation of Mau Mau in *Carcase for Hounds* and *Taste of Death* ("Four Sons of One Father," *Research in African Literatures* 16, Summer 1985, 186).

If Mwangi's adult novels are open to this charge, his children's stories, in which Mau Mau figures significantly, are not. When he began writing for children, Mwangi chose the setting that he knew best from his own childhood: Nanyuki of the 1950s. *Jimi the Dog* (1990) and *Little White Man* (1990) both deal with the adventures of young Kariuki, the son of a cook in the house of the settler farmer Bwana Ruin. While *Jimi the Dog* focuses on how Kariuki gets and raises a puppy, it also addresses issues of social injustice under colonialism. *Little White Man* deals more seriously and in depth with the armed resistance. "I am not certain," Kariuki begins, "when I first heard the word *mau mau*" (1). Mau Mau becomes an integral part of young Kariuki's experience. His friendship and adventures with Nigel, the son of a settler farmer, involve the boys in encounters with freedom fighters in the nearby forest. When Nigel is captured, Kariuki goes to find his friend, only to discover that his brother, Hari, is among the rebels. In a sobering conclusion, Hari is killed by government soldiers after arranging for the release of the two boys. *Little White Man* transcends the genre of the children's story because all of the characters are more complex and nuanced than the relatively caricatured representations in either of Mwangi's Mau Mau adult novels, *Taste of Death* or *Carcase for Hounds*.

In the late 1970s, Mwangi began to write texts that qualified as popular literature. To many of his admirers, these texts were disappointing, lacking the critical edge that had marked his earlier works, especially his urban novels. Mwangi's response to this criticism has been sanguine: He has argued that at this point in Kenya's literary history, it is simply important to provide texts that people will read; since people buy and read popular texts, these are the sort that should be made available. "My only mistake," he has said, "was that I didn't use a pseudonym for my popular novels, and use my own name for the rest. That way I would have avoided all this criticism" (personal communication, 1993). Mwangi did use a pseudonym—David Duchi—for one of his adventure texts, *Assassins on Safari* (1983), but plans with the Longman publishing company for a whole series under this name never materialized.

Mwangi's writing style suits the popular genre. His cinematic vision comes to the fore in the popular novels, which feature spitfire action and frantically paced dialogue. If disappointing when compared with his more serious works, these texts are certainly among the best of their type from Kenya. Mwangi usually takes an event from modern Kenyan or African history or politics as his point of departure: *The*

Bushtrackers (1979) involves poachers in Kenyan game parks; *Bread of Sorrow* (1987) features freedom fighters and diamond smugglers in southern Africa; civil war and famine in the Horn of Africa are found in *Weapon of Hunger* (1989); the South African liberation struggle is presented in *The Return of Shaka* (1989); and *Striving for the Wind* (1990) involves land tenure issues in postcolonial Kenya.

Mwangi's foray into the popular genre began with *The Bushtrackers*, a collaboration with the North American television journalist, Gary Strieker. Film and novel were coordinated to debut together; Strieker created the screenplay, and Mwangi wrote the novel. The story treats one of the better-advertised problems of Kenya in the late 1970s, the decimation of wildlife by poachers. Frank Burkell, a white Englishman, and Johnny Kimathi, a Kikuyu, are park rangers working together in Tsavo Game Park. Johnny retires from this dangerous profession upon marrying and opens a shop on Nairobi's Grogan Road. When the U.S.-based Mafia steps up its ivory-smuggling operations and even breaks into Johnny's store and home because of his refusal to pay "protection" money, Johnny gets mad. He teams up with Frank once again, and amid exciting chase scenes, exploding cars, and fancy shooting, the buddies successfully eliminate the poaching threat and Grogan Road's extortionists in one fell swoop.

Assassins on Safari involves the Kenyan tourist industry and foreign operatives. Kanja, a police reservist turned freelance bodyguard, becomes embroiled in a plan by German mercenaries to assassinate the U.S. Secretary of State during a visit to Kenya's Amboseli Game Park. By foiling the plot, Kanja strikes a blow for Kenyan pride and national sovereignty, proving that the Kenyan police are capable of enforcing the law in their own country. "For the sake of Commissioner Omari and all the other men in our security service who had been made to stand back like little boys and watch the Americans," Kanja concludes, "I was glad I had blundered onto the stage and stolen the show" (163).

Bread of Sorrow would also make an exciting screenplay. It features blackmail, exploding airplanes, gunrunning for South Africa's African National Congress (ANC), diamonds in the mouth of a corpse, Mozambique Liberation Front (FRELIMO) guerrillas, Rastafarians, and spectacular scenery. The action moves from London to Johannesburg to Mozambique to Nanyuki and finally to Msimbati, a small island off the Tanzanian coast. On this island lives Colonel Bridges, an eccentric white man based on the historical figure Leslie Rogers who, after retiring from the East African colonial civil service, settled on a small Tanzanian island, designed his own flag, and declared himself sultan and his island an independent country. Much of the novel is about how the politically conservative South African adventurer Peter Jones comes to side with the ANC.

Weapon of Hunger alludes to the situation in Ethiopia in the mid-1980s. The fictional nation of Borku is experiencing drought and famine, which are exacerbated by civil war in the separatist region of Arakan—a clear reference to Eritrea, which achieved independence from Ethiopia in 1993. Jack Rivers, an American rock star who had raised money for famine relief in the region (an allusion to the Band Aid fundraising and relief efforts of 1985-1986) is concerned that the food supplies are not reaching the famine-struck areas. He organizes a crew of unemployed musicians and makes a daredevil attempt to drive a convoy of one hundred trucks full of food through the desert, spurning government resistance and scorning rebels and bandits.

Of all the popular novels from Kenya, Meja Mwangi's thrillers are among the most creative and the most consistently well written. They nevertheless demonstrate weaknesses present in his other genres. The same inconsistency of detail that Angus Calder, among others, has criticized in Mwangi's novels about Mau Mau arises in his popular texts: plots tend to hinge on far-fetched events, and the fast-paced action and snappy dialogue, usually a plus, at times becomes so clipped as to strain credulity. Mwangi also has a penchant for technical detail: If a character drives a car or flies an airplane, we are sure to be informed precisely what type of car or plane is involved; if a gun is loaded or fired, he states its caliber and describes the precise sound it makes. Although usually effective, this technique misfires when these details are clearly inaccurate or impossibly far-fetched.

As in his other works, the portrayal of women in Mwangi's thrillers is unrelentingly one-dimensional. Almost every Mwangian female serves as the object of male sexual desires. When their usefulness is ended, women are discarded unceremoniously or even brutally. Like cars and guns, they have little importance except as signifiers of male potency and control. Similarly, many of the images and tropes of Africa in Mwangi's thrillers are taken directly from Western narrative and film. This wholesale reproduction of a discourse that treats Africa and Africans in stereotypical and frequently pejorative ways is the most troubling aspect of popular narrative in general and Mwangi's popular works in particular.

Mwangi's novels of the late 1980s and early 1990s, *The Return of Shaka* (1989) and *Striving for the Wind* (1990), occupy ambiguous positions in relation to the rest of his popular works. While they read like popular novels, both endeavor to address serious issues. By this time, Mwangi had clearly demonstrated his ability to write a thriller; however, he also wanted to be considered a serious writer, a sentiment he had expressed at the end of the 1970s. As he explained at the time in an interview with Bernth Lindfors,

> The popular writing can't go on. I mean, one can only write so much on a certain subject before the readers tire and eventually return to the more serious literature. The excitement caused by the emerging popular writing should soon settle down. There is a great future for serious writing here.... I like to develop a serious story in prose. (*Mazungumzo: Interviews with East African Writers* 76, 79)

In fact, Mwangi had already produced serious works in his urban trilogy. But he did not abandon altogether the popular style that had served him so well; *Bread of Sorrow* and *Weapon of Hunger* were published several years after his conversation with Lindfors. This tension between writing styles produced the ambiguities of *The Return of Shaka* and *Striving for the Wind*, which are hybrids of the popular and the serious. While they display many of the same characteristics as Mwangi's thrillers, these novels deal in a much more complex way with contemporary African social issues. At the same time that they draw on some of the tropes of popular writing, they also contain a critical commentary on the genre.

In *The Return of Shaka*, Mwangi takes as his subject the situation of African students in the United States, with whom he had become acquainted during a term with the International Writing Program at the University of Iowa in 1975-1976. As he explains by way of background,

> When I was in the U.S., I met a lot of East Africans in my travels through San Francisco, Washington and Chicago. As we talked, I realized that there was a great need to tell their sad story. I hope to go back and learn more about this situation before finishing this novel. (*Mazungumzo* 76)

As it turns out, Mwangi did not return to the United States, but managed to tell this "sad story" anyway. In it, Moshesh, the son and heir of the traditional leader in a fictional country reminiscent of South Africa, is studying in the United States and plans with a number of his compatriots, also students or professors at U.S. schools, for an armed invasion to liberate his homeland. Backed by generous finances from the father of Moshesh's American girlfriend, the group buys weapons and hires a crack group of mercenaries, who are hanging out in Alabama pool halls. Everything falls apart in the end, however, and it becomes clear that the whole plot was a grand delusion. The anticlimactic conclusion of *The Return of Shaka* contains two serious criticisms: on the one hand, of those African students abroad who compensate for feelings of guilt or failure by inventing elaborate fantasies about their identity and the extent of their patriotic commitment to their homeland; on the other, of the texts that support those fantasies— namely, the popular genre in which Mwangi himself has participated.

Striving for the Wind, another ambiguous text, is Mwangi's most impressive novel since his urban trilogy. While the prose is still snappy and the action fast paced, the story carries a serious message. The novel is set in Mwangi's home area in rural Central Province and concerns the issue of postcolonial land tenure. Baba Pesa (literally, "father of money") is a greedy landowner in the former white highlands who is intent on capturing the remaining parcel of land in his area, which is owned by the poor Baba Baru ("father of dirt"). Pesa's intelligent but disillusioned son, Juda, provides critical commentary. In the end, Baru and Pesa are forced to cooperate and help each other with their harvests, and Pesa rediscovers the cultural and spiritual values of the land, rather than seeing it merely as a source of income. The power of Pesa (money) over Baru (dirt) is weakened. *Striving for the Wind* received honorable mention for the Commonwealth Award in 1991.

Like many other contemporary Kenyan novels, however, the unsatisfactory ending in *Striving for the Wind* fails to resolve the underlying dilemmas raised in the text. The collaboration between Pesa and Baru is endangered by the fact that Baru's daughter, Margaret, is engaged to Juda but has been made pregnant by his father. The full implications of the problem are handily evaded by Margaret's death at the end. As Johansson notes:

> The fact that the endings of some novels are inconsistent with the worlds and characters they construct supports the Jamesonian hypothesis of narrative as a so-

cially symbolic act, aimed at solving an underlying
social contradiction. (124)

Because the underlying contradiction—in this case the divi-
sion of land—is unresolvable in the way the text presents it,
the story is riddled with inconsistencies. To avoid these problems, a text has to address social problems directly—which
was precisely Mwangi's approach in his urban novels.

Meja Mwangi was certainly not the first to write about
the urban setting in Kenya, since that honor accrues to Leonard
Kibera and Charles Mangua, but his urban novels remain the
paradigmatic and in many ways the most interesting examples
of the urban genre from Kenya. Mwangi's urban trilogy offers a riveting account of the constant struggle for survival
that marks life in Nairobi's poorest sectors. *Kill Me Quick*,
Going Down River Road and *The Cockroach Dance* re-cre-
ate landscapes of stinking back alleys and ramshackle dwell-
ings and the severe social problems that accompany them—
inadequate housing and jobs, nonexistent waste-removal services, corrupt officials, alcoholism, thievery and juvenile delinquency. The vivid descriptions of Nairobi's underbelly resemble what has been described as the "excremental vision"
of the Ghanaian writer Ayi Kwei Armah: filth, grime and foul
odors fill the texts.

The urban setting of these novels converts many of
Mwangi's narrative weaknesses into strengths. The individualism that is so tiring in the popular fiction and the Mau Mau
novels is no longer a cliché but a fitting response to the tough
urban setting. The inconsistency of tone and perspective is
less problematic because city life itself is inconsistent. The
portrayal of women, deeply problematic in his popular novels, becomes less objectionable if not yet laudable. Women
are portrayed as sex objects, but then everyone and everything is objectified and prostituted in this dehumanized urban
setting. Mwangi's tales demonstrate the disruption of tradi-

tional structures, including family roles and gender relations, by the urban social milieu.

The main characters in these novels exemplify what Angus Calder has appropriately dubbed the "Mwangian Man," an intelligent, usually well-educated individual whose inability to find a job that uses his skills, or sometimes any job at all, leads him to ever greater cynicism, disillusionment, and despair. Meja in *Kill Me Quick*, Ben in *Going Down River Road*, and Dusman Gonzaga in *The Cockroach Dance* are, despite their differences, classic examples of the Mwangian Man; while Moshesh in *The Return of Shaka* and the young Juda Pesa in *Striving for the Wind* represent a later, if incomplete, return of the Mwangian Man. This character, above all else, has invested Mwangi's writings with their critical edge.

The problems of street children occupy *Kill Me Quick* (1973), the novel that put Mwangi on the East African literary map. With this work, Mwangi tells the fuller story of the "lonely boy" from Kibera's *Voices in the Dark*. The novel is also at least partially autobiographical: Mwangi wrote *Kill Me Quick* after graduating from secondary school and discovering that he and his friends could not find jobs, despite their degrees. *Kill Me Quick* is a first-person narrative in the picaresque tradition. Its protagonists, the adolescent secondary school graduates Meja and Maina, whose names play on the Swahili phonetic rendering of "major" and "minor," represent one of Nairobi's pressing social problems: the growing number of orphaned or destitute boys (and, beginning in the late 1980s, girls as well) who roam Nairobi's streets, surviving through handouts and their wits. In *Kill Me Quick* delinquency leads to involvement with street gangs and more serious crimes; in the end Maina is convicted of murder and will likely hang, while Meja languishes in prison. *Kill Me Quick* won Mwangi the 1974 Jomo Kenyatta Award for Literature, a significant achievement for a first novel.

Going Down River Road (1976) solidified Mwangi's literary reputation, winning him the Kenyatta Award for a second time in 1977. It is the Nairobi novel *par excellence*. In a more deliberate and ultimately more successful manner than in *Kill Me Quick*, Mwangi re-creates Nairobi's backyard, the peripheral areas such as Eastleigh and Mathare Valley that house the disenfranchised and the powerless as well as the River Road area, where Nairobi's inexpensive bars are located. Again, a socially marginal character is the protagonist. Ben is a construction worker on a new addition to Nairobi's growing skyline, the 24-story, ironically named Development House. When the novel opens, Ben has just moved in with Wini, a prostitute and secretary with a son simply known as Baby. The tone (or more accurately, the smell) of the entire novel is established in the novel's memorable opening lines:

> Baby should not have drunk coffee. He urinated all of
> it during the night and now the smell lay thick and
> throat-catching, overcoming even the perfume of his
> mother's bed across the room. In the bed Ben lay with
> the boy's mother curled in his large arms, warm and
> soft and fast asleep. But Ben was not asleep anymore.
> The pungent baby urine stink had awakened him long
> before his usual waking up time. (2)

When Wini deserts them both for a wealthy white man, Ben in a moment of compassion that he occasionally regrets continues to care for Baby. Evicted from Wini's Eastleigh apartment, they take the downwardly mobile step of moving in with Ben's work buddy, Ocholla, in a shantytown shack along the Nairobi River. Eastleigh, a section of Nairobi known for its Somali and Ethiopian refugee populations, at least had solid buildings, but the Nairobi River slum houses an even more destitute population. The impoverished residents of this type of "illegal" settlement are in no position to consider the impossible tasks of acquiring building permits or meeting construction codes when they set up their shacks. The inhabitants are at the mercy of city council extortionists who provide no basic services and burn down the tenants' shacks when they cannot pay "tax" money.

But Mwangi shows that even in Nairobi Valley life is not as bad as it could be. Perhaps the lowest rung on the Nairobi social ladder is represented by another valley slum—Mathare Valley, "the only place in the city where they may keep chickens or perish" (100). In a brilliant passage, Ben passes along the lip of Mathare Valley aboard a city bus on his way to Kariobangi to pick up another supply of *bhang* (marijuana), which he uses to bribe his foreman in order to be assigned more desirable tasks:

> From up here the shanty town appears just as a rubbish heap of paper, scrap iron, dust and smoke. Appearances are deceptive. Down there live enough construction labourers, unlicensed fruit peddlars and illicit liquor brewers to cause concern to the whole city police. It can be nightmarish hunting for vagrants down there. Almost everyone is a vagrant, that is including women and children. And they drink *chang'aa* and smoke *bhang*, two things that cannot stand the sight of a policeman. A few coppers have got themselves knocked cold by unknown assailants down there. Coppers find it easier to follow behind the City Council constabulary who have the right to raze the place down any day in the interest of public health. In the resulting smoke and chaos the policemen descend into the forbidden valley, make a few desperate arrests, then scramble out before the place regenerates into solid, obstinate, granite resistance to law and order. (140)

Mwangi excels in this vivid portrayal of Nairobi's marginal spaces. Morning finds Ben on the roads and paths leading to the city center, along with the crowds of other workers who cannot afford bus fare. No other Kenyan writer has so effectively captured this Sisyphus-like morning ritual that Mwangi describes as an "endless routine trudge, the tramp of the damned at the Persian wheel" (6).

As Mwangi shows, Nairobi is replete with contradictions. Development House, for example, is located on Haile Selassie Avenue at the edge of the financial and business district and next to the site for a new 800-bed tourist hotel. Workers like Ben and Ocholla, who are constructing the building, live in Nairobi's poorest areas; apart from their temporary, low-paying jobs, they are unlikely to benefit from Development House. Mwangi uses the construction of the new building to structure the novel's action: in the first chapter Development House is four stories high; it grows to seven stories by Chapter Seven, thirteen by Chapter Eleven, and its final elevation of twenty-four stories by Chapter Twenty. By contrast, River Road is an area of bars, night clubs and cheap hotels frequented by Nairobi's working classes. Here Ben and Ocholla drink the illegal brews *chang'aa* and *karara*, find prostitutes, and pick fights.

Going Down River Road ends on an ambivalent but predominantly somber note. Mwangi maintains a tentative but fragile hope for the future, as Ben convinces Baby to return to school after a bout of delinquency. Meanwhile, Development House has been completed and the workers are out of a job; but construction of another big building is about to begin. Ocholla's large, hungry family has unexpectedly joined him from their rural home, where the crops have failed and life is hard. Ocholla tells Ben that he and Baby will have to move out. They argue, but as Ocholla runs out of a bar and heads down River Road, Ben chases him as the novel closes: "Ocholla!" Ben hollers hoarsely. "Wait for me; don't leave me here alone. Buddy!" (215).

In many ways, *The Cockroach Dance* (1979) is a perfected remake of *Going Down River Road*. Again, Mwangi has created a buddy story, this time featuring Dusman Gonzaga and Toto, two roommates in Dacca House. Dusman tries to convince himself that this unsightly address on smelly, undesirable Grogan Road is only temporary, but when thieves take the wheels from his car, a broken-down Triumph Herald,

Dusman's last symbol of freedom and possible escape is destroyed. Grogan Road is literally and symbolically adjacent to River Road. The excremental ambience—the bars and brothels, the thieves and cockroaches that operate with equal impunity, the streets filled with drunks, beggars, and survivors—creates a landscape similar to those in Mwangi's other urban novels. Even some of the key images reappear. Compare Dusman's discovery of "a hungry cockroach gnawing at the plastic nozzle of a can of the most reputable insect decimator on the market" (*The Cockroach Dance* 189) to Ben's explanation that "You cannot kill them.... You find them playing with the insecticide container, trying to eat the plastic lid" (*Going Down River Road* 20).

Mwangi again portrays vividly the "tramp of the damned" in Nairobi's underbelly. His preferred metaphor in *The Cockroach Dance*, however, is an embittered version of the Shakespearean notion of life as a drama, rather than the Sisyphus-like image that appeared in *Going Down River Road*. Dusman observes,

> The events that take place daily on these same streets leave you with a dry acid taste in your mouth. Real life dramas, written by an eccentric old bastard having no apparent beginning or end, no winners, only losers and choreographed by a sadistic bitch-goddess. (43)

In *The Cockroach Dance*, Mwangi is as creative as ever, and his humor is as gut-wrenching as his sensory descriptions. Dusman is relatively fortunate for a resident of Grogan Road; he at least has an education and a job. Unfortunately, he belongs to that class of young Nairobians who are overqualified and underemployed. He manifests his frustrations with his dead-end job through fantasies about the parking meters it is his duty to read:

> Dusman Gonzaga had dreamed ... he had become a
> parking meter magnate. He had installed miniature
> meters on the dirty kitchen table for the roaches that
> came in hordes to forage for crumbs. He had invented
> special ones with split-second electronic timing devices
> for the mice and rats out by the garbage cans. (3)

Dusman even invents meters for the vagrants and beggars of downtown Nairobi.

As the novel progresses, cockroaches emerge as the predominant metaphor for Nairobi's derelict populations. *The Cockroach Dance* is, in effect, the story of how Dusman changes his attitude toward these "milling masses" who "sweat sticky, black pitch" (57). His stance is at first reactionary: "Give them a job, force them to work, or take them out and let the army use them as dummies for target practice" (58). But a week of sick leave gives Dusman time to reflect on his experience with Grogan Road and its living conditions. Slowly but surely, he begins to identify with the masses, beginning with "the faceless ones" who inhabit Dacca House. Dusman becomes obsessed with cockroaches, to the point of ordering them in a restaurant. By the end, he is a tentative revolutionary, who concludes that "the wretched of the earth," like tenacious cockroaches that survive despite the odds, "will in the long run prize something out of the tight claws of the not so wretched" (157). Dusman leads the Dacca House tenants, the faceless ones that he once despised, in a rent strike that is still unresolved as the novel closes.

This growth of social awareness is the most important difference between *Going Down River Road* and *The Cockroach Dance*. In *The Cockroach Dance*, Mwangi presents a broader historical and social vision than in all of his earlier work. Nairobi's structure did not suddenly arise overnight; it developed over time, with its roots in the colonial era, as two major narrative interventions on the history and development of Grogan Road testify.

Mwangi's characters are more vivid and memorable than ever in *The Cockroach Dance*. The Swahili names of minor characters show that many of them are deliberate caricatures. The residents of Dacca House include the family of Sukuma Wiki, a vegetable peddlar. *Sukuma wiki*, a green vegetable similar to kale, is commonly eaten with the East African staple *ugali*. The common view of *sukuma wiki* as a budget-stretcher is evidenced by its name, which means "to push the week." In a comic extension, Sukuma's wife is named Vuta (hence, "pull the week"). Chupa na Debe ("bottles and cans") is modeled after real Nairobi residents, who eke out a living by collecting and reselling these items. Mganga ("doctor") is the resident witchdoctor, whose dubious treatments Dusman carefully avoids. Then there is the Bathroom Man, with his wife and child. Dusman's change in attitude toward this family, who lives in a bathroom, is a measure of his changing reaction to the rest of the faceless masses. He finally stops directing his indignation at the family and focuses instead on the real culprit, the landlord Tumbo Kubwa ("big belly").

Clearly, the urban arena has been Mwangi's most successful setting. The five short stories that he has published also deal with urban themes. "An Incident in the Park" (1988), for instance, is about mob justice, an all-too-common occurrence in Nairobi. A vegetable hawker, running from the police who are demanding his license, is accosted by the lunchtime crowd in downtown Uhuru Park and stoned to death. In choosing Uhuru Park as his setting, Mwangi has chosen yet another important space in Nairobi's urban landscape, an area where the unemployed sleep the day away. Only the lunchtime rush of workers hurrying from their government offices downtown and back disrupts the quiet of the park. The incident Mwangi describes in this story succinctly summarizes the issues of alienation and poverty that inform all of his urban texts.

Mwangi's other short stories also present vignettes of urban life. Ben, the construction worker from *Going Down River*

Road, wanders through Nairobi bars in "Like Manna from Heaven" (1974) and meets a sympathetic prostitute in "No Credit: Terms Strictly Cash!" (1976). "I Say Tham" (1975) is reminiscent of *Kill Me Quick*, featuring a shoeshine boy who contracts chronic tuberculosis while in prison. In "Coming Back" (1975) the protagonist, who lives in Nairobi, visits his rural home community and discovers that a former girlfriend has died in a car accident.

Mwangi's urban works offer a new perspective on the tradition-modernity conflict. Characters in Mwangi's Nairobi do not have the luxury of pondering what aspects of traditional life they will keep or reject, or on what terms they are willing to incorporate new social and cultural forms. For people like Meja, Ben and the residents of Dacca House, the primary issue is simply one of survival. In this respect, Mwangi has hit on the most basic crisis of the modern Kenyan city.

Like many writers, Mwangi has expressed frustration with the mixed critical reception he has received, especially for his recent works. The perceived disjuncture between his popular adventure texts and his serious urban novels is a common criticism, and while *Going Down River Road* and *The Cockroach Dance* are generally acknowledged to be his best works, they are inescapably similar to each other. As Calder argues, his writing is characterized by the "unselfconscious deployment of the techniques of 'popular' fiction, which is a source of both weakness and of strength" (G.D. Killam, ed., *The Writing of East and Central Africa*, 177). Mwangi, it seems, needed a new angle to follow up these urban novels.

The Return of Shaka and *Striving for the Wind* represent an attempt both to find that new angle and to create a blend of the popular and serious styles. Concurrent with the publication of these works, Mwangi began publishing his children's stories, a project that, as he explains, resulted from his frustration with the critical reception of his other work. In addition, the children's stories extend his earlier interests. When he was growing up in Nanyuki, Mwangi wrote and illustrated stories to entertain his brother. He has explained his interest in children's writing in terms similar to those used to justify his popular fiction: as an outgrowth of his concern for getting people interested in reading. There is simply not enough written for children from a Kenyan or African perspective.

Mwangi is not alone in his attention to children's literature, since many of Kenya's novelists—Ngugi wa Thiong'o, Asenath Bole Odaga, Marjorie Oludhe Macgoye, David Maillu, and Francis Imbuga, to name a few—have written or are intending to write works for children. It seems logical that in addition to other concerns, Kenyan publishing practicalities may be encouraging this impulse; in the post-Kenyatta years, as we have noted, publishers have curtailed novel production in favor of school texts and children's books.

To be sure, Mwangi's children's stories have been his most successful works in terms of sales, with *Little White Man* being Mwangi's best-selling book of all. The story has been translated into Dutch, French, and German. The German language edition received wide international exposure after being awarded the Deutsche Jugendliteratur Preis in 1992.

Meja Mwangi is unusual among Kenyan writers in that he did not emerge from the university community. Apart from a stint at the University of Iowa as a participant in the International Writing Program, Mwangi had not gone beyond two years of study at Kenyatta University College before establishing himself as a writer. Consequently, when he was awarded a scholarship to pursue a bachelor's degree in English at Leeds University in 1990, he accepted it, partly as a way to remedy what he considered a gap in his experience and partly as an opportunity to take a break from writing. The influence of his university experience on Mwangi's writing remains to be seen. Given his productivity to date and the centrality of his works in Kenya's literary tradition, we are likely to see much more from this particular writer.

Chapter 8

Nyapol's Daughters: Women and the City

Grace Ogot's *The Promised Land* (1966) is the first Kenyan novel written by a woman. The book is also the first Kenyan novel to feature a complex female character and the first to offer a fully sympathetic portrayal of women's concerns. The story opens by introducing the reader to the lonely, frightened Nyapol, newly married and arrived at her husband Ochola's homestead. She listens to the wind and rain from her cold hut:

> Her two bridesmaids, who had stayed with her for the first few weeks, had just left. Before her marriage, Nyapol had never felt loneliness.... But, in this last week, loneliness had crept in. How could she exist in this isolated village? There was not a single woman of her own age.(8)

Nyapol, however, is determined and active. She draws strength from remembering her mother's teaching: that "the act of doing will give you courage" (8). She refuses to conform to the passive role expected of her, in the process challenging traditional assumptions about a wife's proper role. While irreproachable as a hard-working and industrious wife, Nyapol doesn't hesitate to resist her husband's scheme to migrate to Tanzania, lecturing him and even "threatening him with her finger, a thing she had been told never to do to a husband even when she was annoyed" (26). When the move becomes inevitable, she wishes she had never married, observing that her condition constitutes a type of imprisonment (46).

In the end, Nyapol's instincts and actions are vindicated. She is the one to return from Tanzania with her sanity intact, while Ochola loses his possessions and his dignity. Nyapol overcomes her loneliness and fear so that when the final tragedy strikes, she, unlike Ochola, is able to rise above their misfortune. Ochola's domination results in disease and personal disaster, whereas Nyapol ultimately transcends her loneliness and isolation. This is a story, Florence Stratton notes, alluding to Chinua Achebe's famous work, in which *men* fall apart (*Contemporary African Literature and the Politics of Gender*, 1994).

Nyapol stands at the head of a line of strong female characters—Nyapol's daughters, we might call them—who have appeared in novels from Kenya, especially in novels from women writers. While such characters were relatively scarce during the first generation of writers and even during the booming period of the 1970s—*The Promised Land* was an anomaly in this regard—they have multiplied during the post-Kenyatta years. In fact, their appearance may be classified as one of the most significant recent developments in the Kenyan novel.

The important connection between urban space and women's lives is present but understated in Ogot's novel. *The Promised Land* is primarily rural in its setting. Nyapol moves with Ochola from their Nyanza home to another rural setting in Tanzania, before their ignominious return. Many of Nyapol's desires and actions conflict with traditional, rural-based patriarchal structures. Despite the country setting, however, her story presages the potential importance of the city, which is to become so overwhelmingly significant for the later generation of those we are calling Nyapol's daughters. During Nyapol's only encounter with the city—at the harbor in Kisumu, where she watches the dock workers struggling under their loads—she recognizes a relationship between marriage, the city, and the cash economy. Just as men are "bewitched" into accepting the terms of selling their labor in an urban, capitalist market, so are women bewitched into accepting the unfavorable terms of marriage.

In the novels that were to follow *The Promised Land*, and especially those that focus on women and women's issues, the city becomes a central and far more complex symbol. Just as the city represents and comprises obsessions and fears related to other social issues, it is also a signifier of the ambivalent feelings toward gender in contemporary Kenya, in writing from both men and women. Nyapol's daughters, as well as their detractors, all accept the city as the most relevant symbol for the condition of women in Kenya today.

In what would appear to be something of a contradiction, Nairobi has always been an overwhelmingly male domain. Immigration restrictions before World War II meant that the male to female ratio among the African population was nine to one, and even after restrictions were lifted, males continued to outnumber females—at a rate of three to one shortly before independence. Although women's participation in the urban labor force rose from 39 percent in 1977 to 56 percent in 1986, the traditional labor model (i.e., men from rural Kenya work in Nairobi and leave their wives and children at home) is still common.

The nature of the struggle for *uhuru* and the discourse involved in that struggle tended to reinforce this affiliation of women with traditional country life, as women's concerns were subsumed under the overriding conflicts with colonial authorities, which centered on race and class. When missionaries and colonial authorities opposed traditional practices of polygamy and female "circumcision," for example, support for these practices became a rallying point for opposition to colonial rule.

Understandably, most Kenyan women saw their interests resting with the nationalist movement rather than with the colonial authorities, and there were many heroines—sung and unsung—in the struggle against colonial rule. The mother of Gerald Timundu in Kibera's *Voices in the Dark*, an activist in the Mau Mau movement, invokes real-life characters like Me Kitilili and Mary Nyanjiru, whom Ngugi intimates are sources of inspiration for some of his female characters. In a similar and more fully developed vein, Muthoni Likimani's *Passbook Number F.47927* (1985) is a historical work about women's involvement in Mau Mau.

As a result, in the postindependence period, social initiatives that might be in the interests of women have been effectively dismantled by associating them with colonialism. An outstanding example of this phenomenon is the fate of the Affiliation Act, a colonial-era law that held men financially responsible for the maintenance of any children they fathered, regardless of their marital status. In 1968, the Kenyan Parliament rescinded the act. Its reinstatement has been on the agenda of progressive women's groups ever since, but opponents to the Affiliation Act have effectively invoked its origins in colonial policy to sway public opinion against it. By the same token, many feminist initiatives are opposed on the grounds that feminism is a foreign, European concept not appropriate to the Kenyan setting.

Lip service to gender equity in the postcolonial era has rarely resulted in positive and concrete changes for women. Political power remains overwhelmingly male; they have very few female members of parliament, for example. Grace Ogot is herself an exception, having served in parliament as a nominated member, one of the positions appointed by the President. The government has typically ghettoized women's concerns by making them the responsibility of a bureau within the Ministry of Culture and Social Services, in which Ogot served as Assistant Minister. Despite the high profile of the 1985 conference in Nairobi concluding the United Nations Decade for Women, the increased awareness the conference brought did not translate into practical solutions for tackling the root causes of inequality and discrimination.

Gender issues in Kenya are thus rather complicated. If traditional culture is profoundly patriarchal, if the anticolonial struggle was predicated on the validity of traditional values, and if the postindependence city is dominated by men, what is a daughter of Nyapol to do? What Kenya's novels demonstrate first of all are the unique and complex qualities of this dilemma. However, they also suggest that the city, because it disrupts traditional social patterns, and despite its customary nature as a male environment, can be a place where women are able to create some measure of personal emancipation. Women can free themselves from dependence on fathers, husbands, or other men—particularly if they can find employment. The city may be historically male, but it is a complex enough place to allow some maneuvering room for women.

Two real-life events from recent Nairobi history illustrate both the problems and the possibilities that reappear in the novels. The first event—the famous S.M. Otieno case—belongs to the legal realm, and its complexity arises from the fact that Kenya features two sometimes overlapping legal systems: codified law and customary law. In the early colonial years, the British administration transferred the Indian Colonial Legal Code to Kenya, which laid the groundwork for formally codified property rights and land control. At the same time, however, the British policy of indirect rule involved the maintenance of customary law, dispensed through "native" tribunals. There thus emerged a two-tiered legal code with formal, codified law applied to Europeans and customary law applied to Africans (except in those cases where custom was deemed "repugnant" to British law). After independence, the system of separate courts was abolished, but the application of both forms of law has remained.

In 1986, a case appeared before the Kenyan courts that highlighted the interconnections between these two legal systems, the conflict between city and countryside, and gender issues. The case involved the seemingly minor issue of where the body of S.M. Otieno, a prominent Nairobi-based lawyer, should be laid to rest. Both Otieno, a Luo, and his Kikuyu widow, Virginia Wambui Otieno, wanted his body buried on their farm near Nairobi. However, Otieno's family of origin, from the Luo Umira Kager clan, insisted on burial at the family home in Western Kenya, according to custom. The case galvanized unusual public interest and attracted great attention—in some cases, daily coverage—in the Western media as well.

Among other things, this struggle was between the power of rural space, represented by the Umira Kager clan, and urban space, represented by the deceased and his widow. This tension was most clearly evidenced in the discussion during the case over the difference between a house and a home. When the widow's attorney asked one of the plaintiffs whether it were not true that Mr. Otieno had a home in Nairobi, he denied it, replying: "In Nairobi, we have houses and not a home. Even when it is fenced and has a gate, it is a house." The implication clearly was that Nairobi is only a temporary resting place, rather than somewhere one can establish an identity. In the end, Justice Bosire ruled against Otieno's widow and in favor of the Umira Kager clan. Customary law won out over codified law, the rural sphere over the urban, and men over women.

The second event—the flap over the proposed Kenya Times building in Uhuru Park—demonstrates how the power of the (male-dominated) central government over urban space, while strong, is not absolute. In 1989 the ruling party, KANU, which dominates the landscape symbolically through its offices in the most imposing building in the city's skyline, the 28-storey Kenyatta International Conference Center, decided to construct an even larger home. Plans were unveiled for the

Kenya Times Trust building, featuring a central tower of 60 stories, with two 10-story structures on either side and a 10-foot high statue of President Moi in a courtyard. The project was to be financed by loans from the World Bank, with the additional backing of the British media tycoon, Robert Maxwell.

Building plans were announced and rubber-stamped by various official parties, and a ground-breaking ceremony was held—but all in the face of unusually loud protests. Letters to the editor in the major newspapers overwhelmingly opposed the project, which would have effectively destroyed Uhuru Park, a popular lunch spot for city workers. In this case, popular sentiment was articulated most publicly by Wangari Maathai, the leader of the women's environmental group, the Greenbelt Movement. Because of her outspoken opposition, Maathai and her organization became the subjects of harassment and personal attacks by police and politicians. The Greenbelt Movement's headquarters were raided and the group was forced to vacate their offices. Maathai was insulted in widely publicized parliamentary debates in which members of parliament accused her of immorality because of her status as a divorced woman. Despite this onslaught, however, the concerted voices of women and other marginalized groups in Nairobi combined to win this particular contest over a section of Nairobi's urban space.

The stories of Virginia Wambui Otieno and of Wangari Maathai, despite their different outcomes, suggest some of the problems as well as the possibilities for the daughters of Nyapol. Urban geography is the site for their struggles, and it also contains the symbols—residences, skyscrapers and parks, among others—that represent those struggles.

In an impressive analysis of the images of women in African writing, Florence Stratton has pointed out that African men's writing features a ubiquitous trope about women—namely, that woman is an embodiment of African cultures or nations, either as a degraded and corrupt prostitute or as a redemptive virgin. The trope of woman as Mother Africa is not simply an occasional feature of male writing, Stratton insists, it is "one of its *defining* features" (*Contemporary African Literature and the Politics of Gender*, 50). Even those writers, such as Ngugi wa Thiong'o and Sembene Ousmane, who have been praised by feminist critics for their progressive public pronouncements supporting women's rights, participate in an "intertext" or "mastertext" in which the trope is reproduced, she argues. In the case of Kenya, we can certainly see how novelists (such as Thomas Akare and Meja Mwangi, to cite two immediate examples), employ the prostitute figure not as a way to illuminate and explore the problems of women in postcolonial society, but as a grand metaphor for men's (in other words, Kenya's) degradation. What we see is that the city has come to serve as an overloaded symbol in the same way that women have; often, they represent each other.

There are, to be sure, variations in how the Kenyan city is presented with respect to women and women's concerns. In Chapter Six we noted how novels can be described as responding to either hegemonic or counterhegemonic impulses, meaning that their portrayal of society will either support or question the *status quo*. The same type of analysis may be applied to the way texts present gender issues. Hegemonic texts, from the perspective of gender, offer an ideology that supports traditional roles and reinforces the patriarchal order of indigenous Kenyan society. These works are usually, although not exclusively, written by men. Counterhegemonic texts, by contrast, offer ways for the confines of traditional gender roles to be overcome or at least challenged. These are usually, although not exclusively, written by women.

David Maillu, the writer who has contributed so much to the popular genre in Kenya, offers the archetypal hegemonic work when it comes to gender. The rural-urban tensions that form a common thread through the great variety of his writings are analogous to, and generally a metaphor for, another conflict that is a constant in his text: the conflict between men and women in postcolonial African society. The changes in gender roles that were brought by the interrelated social forces of colonialism, missionary activity and urbanization are fundamental in the development of Maillu's plots and themes. The disintegration brought by the city is by this account interchangeable with the disintegration of the traditional roles of men and women, and Maillu's narrative represents a reactionary, hegemonic response to the city.

We noted in Chapter Six how Maillu's most well-known popular work, *After 4:30* (1974), suggests that Emili's only hope for a return to wholeness is in finding a way to replace the absent male in her life. This is accomplished through her son who, because he represents the return of a husband and father, can reconnect Emili to her rural roots and a more stable life. That same ideology is also present in Maillu's more serious, didactic works. Women like the hapless Beatrice Kavele in *The Ayah* (1986) are, like the city, at best shallow and rootless and at worst inherently immoral. Men, meanwhile, even though they are at times implicated in urban evils, are merely its victims. Men are associated with the moral high ground of the rural countryside, but are constantly in danger of succumbing to the seductive lure of the female city.

Such is certainly the message in *Broken Drum* (1991), Maillu's most ambitious work to date in both its historical scope and its sheer size. At 1100 pages, *Broken Drum* is a large tome whose jacket cover unabashedly proclaims it "the longest and greatest novel published in Africa." The storyline has a James Michener scope, following a Kamba family's male line through two centuries of Kenyan history, although the main conflict is between Bonifas Ngewa and his wife Vikirose. Ngewa is interested in getting in touch with his rural Kamba roots, while she is obsessed with the glamour of modern city life. The story opens in Nairobi of the early 1980s, with "another evening rush and push and panic and despair as had become the routine" (1). Commuters are crowding on the buses to go home from work. The connection between the city and women is clear from the start, as Ngewa's mind wanders:

> We are citizens, if anything, only but caretakers of
> this city, thought Ngewa in the traffic . . . Then he
> was thinking about his wife . . . Marriage . . . . (2)

As he thinks, Ngewa drives past a bus stop where men and women struggle with each other to climb aboard. The chaos of the city represents the moral confusion that is caused by and evident in women like Vikirose, and it forms a stark contrast to the order and wholeness of precolonial rural tradition, which the novel idealizes at great length. Ngewa longs for a way to reincorporate the spiritual and social organization of his rural heritage, which is represented through a series of flashbacks featuring his father, grandfather and great-grandfather.

Clearly, the main feature of that heritage is the special place of men in society. Ngewa recalls how things stood during his childhood:

> They were at the *thome* place, an open fireplace at a
> distance from the main house. Here, Nzimba spent
> his evenings chatting with other men and boys, for
> this was an exclusive place for men only. But places
> like this however were getting fewer and fewer these
> days in Akambaland. (40)

The feminization of a society, by this account, weakens it. During the discussions around the *thome*, the topic of the coronation of Queen Elizabeth arises. It is freely predicted that the event signals the decline of the British Empire, since the ascension of a woman to the throne is a sure sign of the decline of power. The narrator concurs that "indeed, it would be during the Queen's reign when the British would lose all its colonies" (*sic*, 44)—handily ignoring that the zenith of British Empire also occurred during the reign of a female sovereign.

The theme unveils itself through a series of interchangeable dichotomies: tradition versus modernity, African practices versus imported practices, the rural area versus the city, and men versus women. In particular, whenever the rural-urban dichotomy is set up, it is soon followed by the male-female parallel. Vikirose is the archetypal Maillu female: seductive and beautiful, but corrupted by materialism and modern, urban ways. Ngewa, for his part, is Maillu's archetypal male. By far Vikirose's intellectual superior, he has been so seduced by her charms that he is unable to pursue his own, "purer" aims. Women, in short, are like the city that has trapped and degraded the African male. Like the city, women are only concerned with surface appearances and with money. Like the city, they are parasites. As Ngewa's friend counsels him,

> Women are traps set in the path of men who want to prosper and in that respect, they are men's greatest enemy . . . . Soft as a woman appears, sweet as she may be, she does not play jokes with a man; for she, like a jigger-flea, lives on the emotions of man and she, like that flea, enters you with a sweet itch and, once inside you, she goes into your bones. A woman comes to you easily like a disease, but does not get out of you easily. (546)

Vikirose and Ngewa have a contentious and stormy relationship. He, despite lapses in fidelity and a strong romantic interest in a young British woman, is always the misunderstood victim, heroically struggling against his selfish, materialistic wife. It is only after a long and turbulent series of sometimes violent disputes that Vikirose ultimately submits to Ngewa's authority. The woman's submission to male control signals a return to stability and normalcy, and the rightful dominance of the rural over the urban, of Machakos over Nairobi. A pastoral paradise is restored in the end.

The admittedly ambiguous opportunities that the city allows for women to escape the restrictions of patriarchal tradition has, perhaps predictably, led to the appearance of what might best be termed "backlash literature." Unlike the standard hegemonic texts like Maillu's, which feature passively stereotypical, caricatured and one-dimensional female figures, backlash literature is characterized by a much more active and even violent reaction to women in nontraditional roles, the strength of which is reminiscent of the attacks on Wangari Maathai's character during the debate over the Kenya Times Trust building. Backlash novels include overt or implied lessons about the personal and social dangers that accompany a flouting of traditional gender roles, and they unequivocally punish the women who do flout them. The most overt examples, not surprisingly, are written by men.

Thomas Akare's *Twilight Woman* (1988), for instance, offers the lesson that women who leave their husbands are likely to end up much worse off than when they began, even if their married life is already in shambles. The characters make frequent and vehement references to the 1985 United Nations Conference, as in this typical interjection: "Are you a tart? Those who were fooled by the Women (*sic*) Conference?" (164). By this account, the problem of the twilight women is that their ideas about freedom from men have backfired, leaving them more destitute and desperate than ever, leaving them only with the option of a life of prostitution.

Other texts offer similar lessons. P.M. Waweru's *Jackie the Ravenous Pest* (1992) punishes Jackie for disobeying tradition (and her father, John Thaka) by failing to be content with enjoying her husband and his wealth, insisting instead that she control them. Waweru's earlier novel, *Judy the Nun* (1990), is equally blatant. Judy rises rapidly from being a primary school teacher to a university professorship, eventually becoming a member of parliament. Despite her spotless character (hence her nickname "the nun"), Judy is ultimately blamed by the narrator for her radical ways. Her independence makes her so hopelessly unattractive that it drives her husband to become a notorious philanderer, "rated among the top sugar-daddies" in the city (196). Shortly after her election, Judy's husband and another parliamentarian shoot each other when the latter attempts to seduce her. Judy, realizing that she has caused all these problems by yielding to her "unnatural" ambitions, forsakes her office and joins a nunnery. The reactionary message is blatant, reinforced by the publisher's blurb that praises the novel as offering "a refreshing side to the women's lib movement."

Such virulently hegemonic texts are by no means the norm, however; even among the novels by men, they are in the minority. In fact, some of the most widely read and influential counterhegemonic narratives from Kenya are written by men. Ngugi wa Thiong'o's *Devil on the Cross* (1982), to cite the most prominent example, has been praised in various quarters for offering an unusually strong heroine, and his earlier *Petals of Blood* (1977) offers the complex figure of Wanja as one of several protagonists. Similarly, Kanaya in Francis Imbuga's *Shrine of Tears* (1993) is a progressive symbol of the cultural energies of the new nation of Kilima, even in her death. In a scene that would certainly remind Kenyan readers of the S.M. Otieno controversy, Kanaya's father insists that she be buried in an area traditionally reserved for men:

> The days of girls and boys are gone. Elders, those days are gone. The days that we now have everywhere in Kilima and elsewhere on this earth are days of children, not of girls or boys. (135)

Women have a new place in society, which is also the message of Koigi wa Wamwere's *A Woman Reborn* (1980), in which Njooki comes to a new understanding of how she has been oppressed by her husband and how his death offers freedom.

In all these cases, however, we still find that the female characters are types rather than fully rounded individuals in their own right. Female characters created by men may be progressive or liberated, but Stratton's thesis still holds: They are more symbolic caricatures than fully developed characters in themselves. Women and the city remain analogous, each representing the other. Even if they are positive tropes, they are tropes nonetheless.

Women's writing is generally counterhegemonic, but we also find that novels by women tend to move beyond the stereotypical tropes described by Stratton. We see more complete, complex characters who illuminate the dilemmas peculiar to women. If the tropes of the first generation of male-dominated writing and those that reappear in the more recent backlash literature tend to work "against the interests of women, excluding them, implicitly if not explicitly, from authorship and citizenship," as Florence Stratton suggests (40), then the task of Nyapol's daughters has been to reinscribe women into authorship and citizenship. Their primary strategy has simply been to tell these stories in more complete ways. By way of rounding out this chapter, we will examine examples from four women novelists: Muthoni Likimani, Asenath Bole Odaga, Margaret Ogola, and Marjorie Oludhe Macgoye.

Muthoni Likimani's novels all concern women's issues in one form or another. *Passbook Number F.47927: Women and Mau Mau in Kenya* (1985) is a historical work about the experience of women during the Emergency, a story that has generally been glossed over in most other novelistic accounts. *They Shall Be Chastised* (1974) examines how the church and mission activities influenced traditional females roles, both positively and negatively. Likimani's first novel, *What Does a Man Want?* (1974) focuses on women's issues in a more recent, postindependence setting.

Published the same year as David Maillu's *After 4:30*, Likimani's *What Does a Man Want?* in fact serves as an excellent companion piece, and in many cases a corrective, to Maillu's story. Both works employ the free verse song style popularized by Okot p'Bitek, although neither matches Okot's *Song of Lawino* in its artistry or poetic merits. Both treat the topics and themes of the newly emerging genre of popular literature, and both properly belong to that genre. What is instructive, however, are their vastly differing perspectives on women and their lives.

Unlike *After 4:30*, which concludes with the message that a woman needs male authority in her life in order to successfully surmount her problems, *What Does a Man Want?* asserts that men themselves are the main problem. The work is structured in thirteen chapters or "parts." The first and last offer a medley of possible answers to the question raised by the title, none of them satisfactory, with each of the intervening parts offering a different case study. As the various women offer their stories, it becomes increasingly clear that no woman can provide what a man wants, even if she could discover what it is. Some are accomplished in the arts of seduction, others are heroically devoted to their husband and family, while still others are exemplary models of hard work and discipline: in all cases, they end up neglected by their husbands.

Likimani's collage provides the unarticulated perspectives of the wives of the philandering businessmen in *After 4:30*; rather than placing the blame on the loose morals of secretaries, as Maillu does, *What Does a Man Want?* shows the men's behavior to be the basic problem. Men's half-hearted appeal to the justification of tradition, with the refrain that "an African man can have as many [wives] / As he wants" rings hollow in all cases (116). All men, it turns out, "Be they your fathers, / Brothers, sons, or husband," are similar in their selfishness and inability to understand their wives (94). Men's betrayal affects not only African women: The book includes the stories of a European woman, an Asian woman, a European woman married to an African man, and an African woman married to a British man. Even after promising starts, husbands regularly neglect their families' material needs and ignore their wives.

If a woman finds satisfaction in raising a child, it is not, as Maillu's text suggests, because that child represents an otherwise absent male figure, but because it validates the woman and mother in her own identity and desires. Unlike the prostitute who lures him away, a wife is no "empty tin" (37). Children offer joy, in contrast to the husband, who lives only for himself and is to be pitied:

> And who is he?
> Stuck in a dark dirty room—
> He has but one life;
> My children have five,
> And my own. (40)

Where Maillu's story posits a return to the land as the palliative for weak womanhood, *What Does a Man Want?* suggests that it is in fact the husband who is weak. It is he (like Ocol in Okot's *Song of Lawino*) who is blinded by the empty glitter of the city. Men are the ones who are fickle, the ones who wind up debilitated by their life of debauchery, succumbing to what Nyapol so astutely identified as the "witchcraft" of the modern economy. Several of the women in Likimani's account mention the unsightly cracks in their feet, which come from working so hard on their homestead. When their husbands show up, they scorn the women for their coarseness but are only too willing to take a share of the money that has been raised on the farm.

One of the speakers in Likimani's work directly upends the thesis of Maillu's *After 4:30*, by suggesting that men can be replaced by land:

> The father of my children
> Lost interest in me complete.
> The *shamba*, now my true companion
> My cattle, chickens, and coffee
> Did cheer me up.
> My children gave me hope

> And alongside the sprouting sucklings
> Expectation was renewed again. (64)

In this way, women create a place in the world and find a way of moving, like Nyapol, from isolation to fulfillment. In one of the closing vignettes of Likimani's book, the speaker, an elderly woman, responds to her husband's demands that she leave, "With simple but firm tongue" that "This is my home! / And my grey hairs / Must here be shaved!" (184).

Were this woman's full story to be told, it might well resemble that found in Asenath Bole Odaga's *Riana* (1991). As a young woman, Riana faces an uphill struggle to maintain her rights and dignity in the face of social structures that would deny her of these. The story is organized around a series of flashbacks, with Riana reminiscing as she sits in her home, treating herself to "a steaming hot mug of coffee made from home roasted, ground coffee beans" (1). She regrets dropping out of school in order to marry Dhimu, who had impressed her with his sophistication and his ability to speak "several European languages" (11). He was, she reflects, like "those heroic well endowed men often featured in some of the paper back romance books which she, like most young girls, enjoyed reading and which provided them with a pleasant escapism" (11). She later discovers that Dhimu has another wife, a German woman named Ulla, with whom he has a son. When Dhimu and Ulla die in a plane crash, Riana refuses to marry any of his relatives, as custom would prescribe. Instead, she marries Sam; and when Sam also betrays her by taking a second wife—by his account, under duress and in compliance with his parents wishes—Riana leaves him.

> Riana reflected and wondered why women had so much on their plates and pots. There was always something cooking for the women and in most cases, not in their favour. (171)

The coffee she prepares for herself, "the way she liked it" (1), indicates her intention to take control of her life and direct it in the manner she chooses.

Like David Maillu, Asenath Bole Odaga is a prolific writer who works in a variety of genres, most notably novels and children's stories; like Maillu, she established her own publishing establishment, the Kisumu-based Lake Publishers and Enterprises, as an outlet for her and others' creative works. Unlike Maillu, however, her works offer complex female characters who are more than simplistic symbols of social ills. Women like Riana labor under the dual burdens of traditional patriarchal practices and economic disenfranchisement. Just as Likimani offers a female perspective on the dynamics presented in Maillu's *After 4:30*, Riana's story is a corrective to Maillu's one-sided presentation of Vikirose in *The Broken Drum*. Where Maillu shows Ngewa's affair with a white woman to be at worst a harmless escapade, Odaga suggests that the tradition Ngewa appeals to is merely a pretext for betrayal.

Margaret Ogola sketches an even more recent portrait of Nyapol's daughters in her first novel, *The River and the Source* (1994). Again, a comparison to Maillu's *Broken Drum* is instructive, for, like Maillu, Ogola has created a narrative of epic scope in covering four generations of a Kenyan family, in this case a Luo family. Unlike Maillu, however, the focus of this story is on the women of the family; it is they, in the end, who maintain the tradition and dignity of the family line.

If *Broken Drum* promotes a return to traditional gender relations, *The River and the Source* shows that those relations can be unfavorable for women. Chief Odero's daughter, Akoko, is the remarkable protagonist in this story. Like Nyapol, she is an irreproachable wife who conforms to the requirements of *chik* (tradition). She is even more blunt than Nyapol, however, in articulating the difficulties some of these customs present for women. When her husband dies and his lazy brother takes over as chief, using his authority to enrich himself at her expense, she feels "the weight of injustice that women have felt since time immemorial in her male dominated world" (66). Her daughter, Nyabera, winds up in a similar predicament when her husband dies: "To be a widow and young was an untenable situation" (91). Men of course have no reason to question *chik*, but here, Nyabera finds, is a situation where it "had erred, the first time such a thought had ever passed through her mind" (91).

Akoko finds support where she can: from her family (to which she returns after her mother-in-law insults her) and from the newly established colonial authorities. Significantly, it is to the city—Kisumu, the seat of local colonial rule—where Akoko goes to redress her most serious grievances with her brother-in-law; her epic trip results in his overthrow and a limited measure of emancipation for her. In the same way, her daughter Nyabera finds a certain freedom and inspiration at the mission station. As the narrator describes it, Nyabera is attracted to Catholicism because of the important role of Mary, after whom she is christened: "A woman! One would think that he would have chosen to be born of the unilateral efforts of a man; but no, a woman it was" (97).

The River and the Source offers an intergenerational family line focused on and eulogizing its female members. In this case, it is the men who are tropes, caricatures, or static symbols: Akoko's father is a respectable chief, but he dies early on; her husband, also an honorable man, dies after "mysteriously ailing"; Nyawera's son takes himself out of the family line, as far as reproducing that line goes, by becoming a priest. In this narrative, the amount of respect that is due to men is directly proportional to how well they treat women. It is Akoko's father, Chief Odero himself, who provides the story's title when he comes to realize that "a home without daughters is like a spring without a source" (9). Akoko's husband is also good because of his refusal to take another wife. Akoko's brother-in-law, by contrast, is despicable because he treats his many wives "like sluts." Awiti's husband Mark, on the other hand, helps with the housework. The real heroes are the women: Akoko, her daughter Maria Nyawera, her granddaughter Elizabeth Awiti, her great-granddaughter Veronica, and the great river of descendants who follow.

Taken as a group, the richest collection of female characters in all of Kenyan literature is to be found in the novels of Marjorie Oludhe Macgoye. Although they are deeply evocative of broader issues of nationalism and national development, Macgoye's female characters are never made to carry the entire burden of that representation. Women in Macgoye's work can serve as symbols of nationhood, but they are also much more. These women—Lois Akinyi (*Murder in Majengo*, 1972), Paulina (*Coming to Birth*, 1986), Wairimu, Rahel and Sophia (*The Present Moment*, 1987), and the eponymous Victoria (1993, in a prequel to *Murder in Majengo*)—are the most complex and compelling in contemporary Kenyan writing.

Macgoye's first novel poses as a thriller, but *Murder in Majengo* (1972) is more accurately a commentary about urban poverty in Kenya during its first decade of political independence. Macgoye is especially interested in the social dynamics of the city and the slums. Majengo (which literally translated means "buildings") is the common term for the earliest slum areas of Nairobi and—in the case of this novel—Kisumu.

Macgoye's subsequent novel, *Coming to Birth* (1986), offers an insider's view of similar issues. When Paulina first moves to Nairobi to join her husband she is young, inexperienced, and powerless. The setting of the novel is the Nairobi of the Mau Mau Emergency; Paulina's husband, Martin, has been able to secure a room in Pumwani because the colonial administration's "Operation Anvil" had recently cleared out many of its Kikuyu residents.

The title evokes several layers of meaning, the most obvious being Paulina's difficult pregnancies. She has a miscarriage shortly after arriving in Nairobi, and several more throughout her life. The son she does have is tragically killed by a stray bullet during riots protesting President Kenyatta's visit to Kisumu. In the end, after being reunited with Martin, she is expecting another child. The nurse tells her,

> Take your card to door number three. She always does her best for people like you, people who have cherished their hope for a long time. I hope for you too. (150)

This impending birth at the novel's close offers a second layer of meaning: the birth of a new nation and the hopes for a new and better society. Interwoven throughout the story are the high and low points of postcolonial Kenyan history, including the euphoria of *uhuru*, the politically motivated assassinations of Pio Gama Pinto, Tom Mboya, and J.M. Kariuki, and the arrests of the writer Ngugi wa Thiong'o and the politicians Seroney and Shikuku.

The third and most important coming to birth, however, is the maturation of Paulina herself. From the shy and sickly country girl who steps off the train at the novel's opening— "thinner than he remembered . . . and pale, with deep shadows under the eyes" (2)—she develops into a confident, independent, and self-assured woman. Although it is by no means easy, the city offers Paulina the space in which to improve her life. There she can by-pass traditional expectations and take at least partial control of her destiny. She is able to leave Martin when he mistreats her and learns new skills through vocational education courses. In the end, Paulina has established herself in modest accommodations as the housemaid for a wealthy but progressive family, and Martin even moves in to live with her—the exact reverse of the scene at the opening of the book and a sharp departure from traditional Luo expectations. As the story closes, Paulina is connected to a strong female community in this otherwise male-dominated city. As her friend Amina insists, the city allows a chance for women to "*make* what comes, and *take* the best of it" (146), rather than the other way around.

Like Macgoye's other novels, *The Present Moment* (1987) features a disenfranchised female community, in this instance a group of destitute elderly women living in a church-run home in Eastleigh known simply as "the Refuge." Like her other novels, this one highlights the story of Kenya's development as a nation by interweaving the personal lives of the women—who come from all parts of the country and are a microcosm of Kenyan society—in a complex series of flashbacks, dreams and reminiscences. Like Macgoye's other novels, *The Present Moment* points to the city as the birthplace of a new, albeit uncertain, nation.

The development of a significant tradition of writing by women is one of the most important recent developments in Kenya's literary history. The female characters in writing by women offer new perspectives and revised accounts of Kenyan women's stories. Often these may be read as direct retellings of those women's lives that are presented so very differently, usually inadequately, in hegemonic writing from men. Nyapol and her daughters have had to overcome the burdens of isolation and loneliness and frequent betrayal by the men who wield so much power in their lives. Interestingly enough, these works show that the city—despite its frequent characterization as a place of loneliness, corruption, and despair—offers women, as often as not, the opportunity to overcome the loneliness, passivity, and betrayal that have plagued them.

Chapter 9

Conclusions: The City and the Postcolonial Imagination

A comprehensive overview of the Kenyan novel reveals that the city has fired the postcolonial literary imagination in a way that no other single symbol or idea has. This should perhaps not surprise us. Even though Kenya is still predominantly rural, urbanization is one of the most important social developments of the twentieth century, and is only likely to increase in significance. It is not overstating the case to assert that in sub-Saharan Africa the city is in a condition of crisis, beset by all manner of social problems, but like any crisis simultaneously offering unique opportunities.

The city and the novel have a close and unique link in postcolonial Kenya. The conflicts between traditional and imported ways of life have been the dominant concern of Kenyan and other postcolonial writers; almost without exception, these writers have adopted the city as both site and symbol of those conflicts in their texts. In addition, it may be argued that the novel replicates on the level of cultural production many of the same dynamics as the city. Like the city, the novel is a recently imported form, and like the city, the novel is a wrestling ground, in which expectations rooted in indigenous tradition and expectations raised by "modern" importations struggle with each other.

It is important to avoid the concept of the postcolonial city as a "juvenile" or "immature" form of a European city, just as it is important to avoid viewing the postcolonial novel as an "underdeveloped" form in relation to European literature. We must reject the notion that the African city (or the African novel) simply recapitulates the stages of European urban development (or literary development) only on a later timetable. This kind of recapitulation model overlooks the important contextual differences between eighteenth century England where the British novel began and twentieth century East Africa, where the Kenyan novel began. Both the postcolonial city and the postcolonial novel are specifically twentieth-century phenomena. The "political unconscious" of the city and the novel alike are a function of East Africa's position on the periphery of the world economy, in which traditional, non-capitalist elements retain significant strength. The contradictions and tensions that we read in such places as the troubled endings of Kenyan novels or in the ambivalence between serious and popular writing are a manifestation of those tensions.

In the process of exploring these issues, I hope I have highlighted the scope and variety of novels coming from Kenya, as well as some of the constraints and challenges facing contemporary writers in this country. If the task of artists is to provide a society with the stories and myths that help make sense of their society, one of the major challenges for Kenyan writers in the immediate postcolonial era has been to provide a new set of stories and a new set of myths to help Kenyans understand the meaning of a place like Nairobi and to deal with the challenges of living in such a place. In the process, Kenyan writers have provided an analysis of urban social dynamics, explaining and presenting the city in a variety of ways.

Nairobi has many faces, depending on whose version of the city one reads. Nairobi is a playground for the new generation of African entrepreneurs (Maillu, Ruheni); it is where that same generation becomes embroiled in conflicts and power struggles that sometimes get out of control (Ndissio-Otieno); Nairoi is a melting pot for a new post-ethnic Kenyan paradise (Dawood); Nairobi is the ultimate coming-of-age initiation rite (dae Mude); Nairobi is the site of betrayal and disillusion-ment (Githinji); Nairobi is a place that will make you take your own life (Wambakha); Nairobi is a dark and oppressive place (Kibera); on the other hand, Nairobi is where the lights burn bright and where a fast-thinking person can make a for-tune (Mangua, Kiriamiti); Nairobi is where flawed individuals struggle to make the best of their limited resources and knowl-edge (Macgoye).

One of the most interesting developments that we have observed is the city's function in relation to men and women's roles. Clearly, the city offers an alternative to the traditional patterns of gender relations, and the different portraits of the city in this regard are telling. On the one hand are a group of texts that I have labelled "backlash" literature, which empha-sizes the corruption and degradation of the city, and which genders it female. The best symbol for Nairobi, by these ac-counts, is the prostitute. David Maillu's texts are among the most consistent in presenting this hegemonic message: The innocent country girl Beatrice (in *The Ayah*) and the hardened prostitute Emili (in *After 4:30*) both need to learn essentially the same lesson, which is that only through a return to the countryside and to the traditional female roles found there, will they be saved. The most outrageous novels in this re-gard, however, are from Peter Waweru: *Judy the Nun* and *Jackie the Ravenous Pest* present strong, ambitious women who in the end are either punished or meekly return to their "proper" roles.

In contrast to these texts are stories from writers like Marjorie Macgoye or Asenath Odaga, in which the city offers some hope for women, allowing them to create a space for themselves in ways that the patriarchy of rural social structures cannot. Even though these writers may not espouse the overt rhetoric of feminism in their personal lives (and, in fact, they do not), their texts contain a feminist vision of the city that makes room for alternatives.

Throughout, I have asserted that the most important overriding tension in contemporary Kenyan narrative is the dichotomy between tradition and modernity and that this dichotomy is manifested most fully in the city. This assertion is challenged, however, by precisely those works that I have highlighted as being Kenya's paradigmatic city novels: Meja Mwangi's urban trilogy. For the characters in *Kill Me Quick*, *Going Down River Road*, and *The Cockroach Dance*, the entire tradition-modernity conflict seems irrelevant. Mwangi's protagonists—Meja, Ben, and Dusman—spend precious little time agonizing about how to appropriately reconcile indigenous practices from the rural areas with their urban lives. Ocholla and the Bathroom Man do not lie awake at night wondering whether or not the cultural practices of their heritage are being lost. For these characters, as for so many denizens of cities like Nairobi, the key issue is simply surviving. To return to Mwangi's metaphor, city dwellers are reduced to cockroaches, scuttling about in a frantic dance of survival. They have neither the time nor the energy to bother with questions of cultural integrity.

What, then, is the connection between Mwangi's urban novels and the more esoteric issues of tradition, modernity, and cultural forms that we have raised in relation to other texts? The answer, I am suggesting, may be found in a historical and especially a geographical perspective. Mwangi's urban novels force us to ask why conditions in Nairobi stand as they do. By looking again at the position of the postcolonial city in the broader global context, by looking again at the historical function of the city in the East African region, we are forced to ask ourselves about the reasons behind the hopeless situations faced by Meja, Ben, and Dusman. The poverty and squalor in Mwangi's urban novels bring us back to the root of the problem, which is economic, and Mwangi's texts may be called paradigmatic because in their narrative they expose this basic reality in a fundamental manner. *Kill Me Quick*, *Going Down River Road*, and *The Cockroach Dance* are an indictment of the neocolonial social structures of the city that reduce people to cockroaches.

The texts that we have examined in this study represent the first thirty-five years, or the first generation, of postcolonial Kenyan writing in English. As we enter the second generation, at the start of the twenty-first century, it seems likely that the African city will continue to be the most important site and symbol of social change on the continent. Writers will continue to discuss, analyze, and affect our understandings of the urban landscape in conscious and unconscious ways.

Part III

The Novels

An Annotated Bibliography of the Kenyan Novel

Adalla, Carolyne. *Confessions of an AIDS Victim*. East African Educational Publishers, 1993. Spear Books.

> An epistolary confessional, in which Catherine explains to her friend Marilyn that the blood test she took, in order to be admitted as a student in the United States, showed her to be HIV positive. Her retrospective insights include treatises on the symptoms and causes of AIDS, sex education in Kenyan families and schools, gender issues, the immaturity of university students, and intertribal love relationships.

Akare, Thomas. *The Slums*. Nairobi: Heinemann, 1981.

> Young Eddy "Chura" Onyango ekes out a living by washing cars in the Majengo slums, where he and his friends survive by sleeping in abandoned cars, scraping by with the help of drinks and drugs. Through Eddy we are introduced to Nairobi's ugly underbelly. When his "home" (an abandoned Zephyr) is towed away, along with his GCE certificate, Eddy gives up all hope. He plans to commit a robbery, turn himself in to the police, and live in the relative security of jail for the rest of his life. The novel ends as he is running toward the police,

the crowd behind him raising the cry of alarm. Perhaps he makes it, or perhaps he falls victim to the mob justice seen elsewhere in the text.

Akare, Thomas. *Twilight Woman*. Nairobi: Heinemann, 1988. Spear Books.

> Resila joins her husband in Nairobi but is soon disillusioned by his quality of life. She was expecting much better. When she runs off with Arthur and he later dumps her, she becomes a prostitute, one of Nairobi's "twilight women."

Allan, Maina. *One by One*. Nairobi: Comb Books, 1975.

> The revelations of a village nymphomaniac. Published "with a touch by David G. Maillu."

Alot, Magaga. *A Girl Cannot Go On Laughing All the Time*. Nairobi: Heinemann, 1975. Spear Books.

> Dave's girlfriend, Edna, throws him out when he pursues an affair with Jeanine. She, meanwhile, finds a rich German tourist. This short text portrays Nairobi as a place of fast-paced living, of instability and corruption, and of quick and sudden death. Nairobi is a place where "those who make mistakes or can't take the heat fall by the wayside" (1).

Asalache, Khadambi. *A Calabash of Life*. London: Longman, 1967.

> In a precolonial Luhya setting, the protagonist Shiyuka sets out to reclaim the usurped chieftainship of the Vatirichi for his family line. His love for Ayako, "a girl from a respected family," spurs him on.

Bobito, Jennifer. *Prescription: Love*. Nairobi: Transafrica, 1975. Afromance.

> Romantic intrigue breaks out in the hospital as the new nurse, Mary Sabala, wins the respect and finally the love of the reserved Dr. Mapena.

Bundeh, Benjamin Garth. *Birds of Kamiti*. Nairobi: Heinemann, 1991. Spear Books.

> One of the "my life in crime" genre, this is Bundeh's autobiographical account of being jailed for a crime he did not commit. The story centers on both the preamble to his trial and on the appeal in which he defends himself and wins. The text includes photos and an appended copy of the court of appeals judgment.

Butere Girls High School, Form IVA. *Loice: High School Student*. Nairobi: East African Publishing House, 1970.

> The story of Loice's experience at Putapwa High School from her entrance as a first-year student through graduation. Written by the 1968 Form IV class at Butere Girls High School, presumably with some editorial assistance from the school staff, the style is reminiscent of English juvenile fiction.

Buyu, Mathew Osunga. *A Thousand Fireflies*. Nairobi: Longman, 1974.

> Because Esta's parents are devoutly religious, they drive her from their home when she becomes pregnant. Esta dies in childbirth, assisted only by her lover Noah. In the end, things are bleak for everyone; even the few fireflies in the cold and the dark seem insignificant.

Chahilu, Bernard P. *The Herdsman's Daughter*. Nairobi: East African Publishing House, 1974.

> A coming-of-age story about Rebecca Embunzi, daughter of a rural Luhya farmer. When she is falsely accused of running away with the local headmaster, she decides to flee the community where she is now disgraced. She boards a bus for Nairobi.

Cuthbert, Valerie. *The Great Siege of Fort Jesus: An Historical Novel*. Nairobi: East African Publishing House, 1970.

> One of the main historical buildings in Mombasa is Fort Jesus, which was originally built by the Portuguese at the end of the sixteenth century. The fort changed hands numerous times during its history. Cuthbert's story is a fictional re-enactment of the siege and eventual conquering of the fort by the Omani Arabs in 1698.

Cuthbert, Valerie. *Dust and the Shadow*. Nairobi: Phoenix Publishers, 1990.

> A historical novel about the people of Shuk, who migrate through the Rift Valley in search of a resting place in the promised land of Ophir. Author Valerie Cuthbert, a long-time Mombasa resident, writes the "Mombasa Notebook" column for the *Daily Nation* from her home on the coast.

Davin, Diarmuid and Pity Wamuhu. *The Trials of Nero Okamba*. London: Macmillan, 1993.

> The story of a struggling middle-class family living in the capital city of the fictional nation of Majini. Nero Okamba is a high school teacher and his wife a civil servant. Their lives are disrupted when Nero is arrested

on trumped-up charges of belonging to the illegal anti-government People's Action Movement.

Dawood, Yusuf. *No Strings Attached.* Nairobi: Heinemann, 1978. Spear Books.

Dawood's first novel centers on Dr. Ahmed, who sets up a practice in Kenya after his medical training in England. The plot proceeds along a series of dramatic anecdotes having to do with medical dilemmas and their solutions.

Dawood, Yusuf. *The Price of Living.* Nairobi: Longman, 1983.

Maina Karanja is a Kikuyu businessman who has made a fortune in the food processing business. When his archrival, Wahome, tries to capture the market with a new product Karanja has introduced, we are treated to a variety of boardroom maneuvers that are not always entirely legal.

Dawood, Yusuf. *One Life Too Many.* Nairobi: Longman, 1987.

Sydney Walker has spent most of his life in Kenya, working first in insurance and later in the tourist industry. Charles Gethi, a member of the new Kenyan economic elite, is the director of the board for the company where Sydney works. Sydney's marriage, divorce, remarriage, and his death in an alcohol-related car crash form the basis of the story.

Dawood, Yusuf. *Yesterday, Today and Tomorrow.* Nairobi: Longman, 1987.

An autobiographical account of Dawood's life in three countries: his country of origin, India; the site of his medical training, England; and his chosen homeland where he pursues a medical career, Kenya.

Dawood, Yusuf. *Off My Chest*. Nairobi: Longman, 1988.

An account of Dawood's life and career in Kenya, beginning with his arrival in Nairobi in 1961 to work at the Aga Khan hospital. Dawood emphasizes the interest in "human nature" that drives both his surgical and writing careers. A collection of anecdotal accounts of his experiences as a physician and surgeon in Kenya.

Dawood, Yusuf. *Water Under the Bridge*. Nairobi: Longman, 1991.

Divided into three sections representing each decade since Kenya's independence, this novel traces the history of three families—one Asian, one Kenyan, and one European—through the postindependence era. The text argues that isolation and prejudice have given way to tolerance and a genuinely multiracial Kenyan society. This is Dawood's most ambitious work to date, and features the usual scenes and characters from the Dawood's own medical profession. Of note is the reference to AIDS, a new disease in Nairobi that kills one of the lead characters.

Dawood, Yusuf. *Behind the Mask*. Nairobi: Longman, 1995.

Dawood's third collection of surgical anecdotes, which he suggests in his Preface will be "perhaps, the final volume in the series."

Duchi, David (Meja Mwangi). *Assassins on Safari.* Nairobi: Longman, 1983.

> A thriller set in the Kenyan game parks. Kanja, a police reservist turned freelance bodyguard, becomes embroiled in a plan by German mercenaries to assassinate the visiting U.S. Secretary of State during his visit to Amboseli Game Park.

Genga-Idowu, F.M. *Lady in Chains.* Nairobi: East African Educational Publishers, 1993. Spear Books.

> Ochola takes his family to Nairobi, where life is hard. His wife works in a bar to support the family, and eventually his attractive wife, Sue, is "rented" out to a wealthy young man. She grows enamoured of a life of riches; in the end, the jewelry and chains entrap her, and she refuses to return to her old life.

Geteria, Wamugunda. *Black Gold of Chepkube.* Nairobi: Heinemann, 1985. Spear Books.

> World coffee prices rose sharply in the mid-1970s, thanks to a severe frost in the coffee-growing regions of South America. A large smuggling operation was set up on the Kenya-Uganda border so that Ugandan farmers could get their product to market. John Kimaru, a District Assistant in Western Kenya, cashes in on the trade in "black gold" in the border town of Chepkube.

Geteria, Wamugunda. *Nice People.* Nairobi: African Artefacts, 1992.

> Dr. Joseph Munguti sets up shop as a "venereologist" in a River Road clinic, where he pursues his personal crusade to lessen the stigma of venereal diseases. If

they can be discussed more openly, he believes, treatment will be more successful. The story contrasts the altruistic but philandering Munguti with a money-grubbing group of doctors who set up an AIDS clinic for the rich. The text raises various issues in medical ethics, including the controversy over sex education in the schools and the AIDS epidemic. The novel was inspired in part by an article from former *Washington Post* reporter Blaine Harden, which, in addition to outlining the serious nature of AIDS in East Africa, also quotes a World Health Organization official who suggests that part of the disease's danger comes from the belief that "nice people" are not at risk.

Gicheru, Mwangi. *The Ivory Merchant*. Nairobi: Heinemann, 1976. Spear Books.

Komu, the Ivory Merchant, links up with John Murimi in the illegal ivory trade. But things get complicated, as they begin competing with one another and the forces of the law, making life dangerous for them both.

Gicheru, Mwangi. *Across the Bridge*. Nairobi: Longman, 1979.

Kahuthu, a "top civil servant" employs a houseboy, Chuma, who seduces his daughter Caroline and "crosses the bridge" of class divisions. When Caroline becomes pregnant, however, Chuma runs away, leading to a long string of events in which Chuma is involved in a bank robbery and thrown into jail. In the end Chuma repents, and he and Caroline are reunited in genuine love.

Gicheru, Mwangi. *The Double-Cross*. Nairobi: Longman, 1983.

> The Nairobi businessman Lodi Karafuu becomes involved in the smuggling of foreign currency out of Kenya. He runs into danger when he tries to double-cross "the Wiper."

Gicheru, Mwangi. *Two in One*. Nairobi: Longman, 1984.

> When Halili realizes that she is unable to have children, she resorts to stealing babies and raising them as her own. The inspiration for the story, according to the book's epigraph, was the abduction of the author's own daughter and his subsequent discovery of a string of baby-snatching stories. The story highlights the question of ethnic identity, since Halili's children all come from different parts of Kenya. The Nairobi International Show—an event that attracts Kenyans from all over the country—is where Halili's trick begins to come unraveled.

Gicheru, Mwangi. *The Mixers*. Nairobi: Longman, 1991. Masterpiece series.

> A story of racial conflict in the White Highlands during the two to three decades before independence. When the wife of farmer Victor Robinson dies, he marries his Kikuyu house-servant Lillian, and the "mixer" family is born. Crucial to the tale are the reactions from the colonial settler community, the "white man's haven and black man's hell" that is Nairobi, and the Mau Mau conflict.

Gitau, Wairimu Kibugi. *Beyond the Cultural Barrier*. Nairobi: Wairiumi Kibugi Gitau, 1993.

> Kenya's era of independence has just begun, but Susan Wanja's ends when she moves from her grandmother's house to join her father and stepmother in Mombasa, where she is treated cruelly. She leaves to work as an *ayah* for a white farm family in Kikambala. Later, she moves to Nairobi to study nursing. Her affections are torn between her childhood friend, Suleiman, and the young Englishman, Richard Randall. Surprisingly, her stepmother helps convince the family that a cross-cultural marriage is acceptable.

Gitau, Wairimu Kibugi. *Together We'll Start a New Life*. Nairobi: Wairimu wa Kibugi, 1996.

> In 1992, a Kenya Air Force plane crashed in Nairobi's Kaloleni Estate, killing about 50 people. This novel tells the story of Lucy Mugure, a teenage schoolgirl who loses her family in the crash and is left in the care of an aging grandmother and a grumpy aunt. When Dr. Muriuki, who had been paying attention to her, marries Lucy's teacher, she is disappointed, but death strikes again, leaving Muriuki free to marry Lucy after all.

Githae, Charles Kahihu. *A Worm in the Head*. Nairobi: Heinemann, 1987. Spear Books.

> In this popular adventure tale in the tradition of Mangua's *Son of Woman*, we follow the life of Fred, a Grade II mechanic in Nakuru whose life is action-packed. Fred lives with the reckless abandon of "a goat with a worm in its head," giving the book its title.

Githae, Charles Kahihu. *Comrade Inmate*. Nairobi: East African Educational Publishers, 1994. Spear Books.

> Fred Wamatu is in jail, charged with attacking and crippling his Kariokor roommate. His colleagues include a judge, a member of parliament, a doctor, and a priest. Their stories make up the bulk of the novel.

Githinji, Sam. *Recovering Without Treatment*. Nairobi: Kenya Literature Bureau, 1981.

> Munyaga's family is a "more or less typical Kikuyu family" in the years leading up to the Emergency. He is arrested as a Mau Mau suspect. On his release, he helps to reconcile friends divided by the Mau Mau experience.

Githinji, Sam. *Struggling for Survival*. Nairobi: Kenya Literature Bureau, 1983.

> Kamau, a laborer and squatter on the large highland farm of Mr. Smith, is forced to leave with his family when their house is burned. Kamau's investment in a cooperative society's project to buy and distribute a settler's farm is lost when the cooperative's director swindles the members and seizes the farm for himself. The story highlights the corruption of the postindependence elite and the breakdown of family traditions and values in an increasingly urbanized postcolonial Kenya.

Gitimu, Chris N. *The Biting Lips*. Nakuru: New-Age Publishers, 1985.

> Peter Muiru works in an office in Thika, his dull life varied only by his frequent love affairs. Things rapidly

deteriorate, however. He loses his job and is arrested for attempted burglary.

Hinga, Edward. *Sincerity Divorced*. Nairobi: East African Literature Bureau, 1970.

> Njamiki, in a moment of sincerity, confesses to her husband Hinga the shocking realities of her life, including her affairs, her drunkenness, and her plans to murder him. In his anger, Hinga drives Njamiki and their daugher out of the house. Winner of a Students' Book-Writing Scheme award.

Hinga, Edward. *Out of the Jungle*. Nairobi: East African Literature Bureau, 1973.

> Kiamba is arrested on false charges and tortured as a Mau Mau suspect. He only manages to escape his prison camp after a long ordeal. The situation facing those he leaves behind, especially his family, is grim.

Holi, D. *Breaking Chains*. Nairobi: Heinemann, 1989.

> Young Ali, a fourteen-year-old living near Lamu, dreams of an adventurous life and joins a gang of smugglers. He is also in search of his unknown father.

Imbuga, Francis. *Shrine of Tears*. Nairobi: Longman, 1993.

> Jay Boge is a new graduate of the national university in Kilima. The death of his girlfriend Kanaya forces him to confront the issues of cultural imperialism that he had been pondering throughout his studies. The charismatic figure of Headmaster is an inspiration to Boge and his agemates.

Irungu, James. *The Lost Generation.* London: Macmillan, 1985. Pacesetters.

Cecily Wanjama helps the police bust a Nairobi drug gang. In the process, she and her friends learn important lessons: crime does not pay.

Irungu, James. *Circle of Betrayal.* London: Macmillan, 1987. Pacesetters.

Wahomeh, a talented engineer and civil servant, is accused of betraying Njeri and her father by squandering their assets. Against the obvious evidence, Njeri refuses to believe Wahomeh capable of such deeds, and in the end her trust is rewarded with love and money.

Irungu, James and James Shimanyala. *The Border Runners.* London: Macmillan, 1984. Pacesetters.

When Waichari's parents die in a car crash, leaving behind huge debts and younger children for Waichari to take care of, he tries smuggling coffee through the Ugandan border town of Chepkube in order to raise money to prevent the sale of the family farm.

Irungu, James and James Shimanyala. *Operation Rhino.* Nairobi: Macmillan, 1989.

High-placed politicians are part of a poaching and smuggling network that is exporting rhino horns. The minister of wildlife recruits a multinational team to capture the poachers.

Juma, Para (Peter Okondo). *Portait of Apartheid: An Historical Novel.* Nairobi: East African Publishing House, 1979.

Onalo Magyo leaves Mombasa for South Africa in order to pursue his education, but he soon comes up against the violent realities of apartheid. His friendship with a young white woman, Betty Borner, is a symbol of hope for interracial harmony in that setting.

Kagiri, Samuel. *Leave Us Alone*. Nairobi: East African Publishing House, 1975.

The aging Kamani tells a tale from his childhood in colonial Kenya: When his friend Wamaitha refused to be circumcised, she faced the wrath of the community. She, Kamani, and their friend Gathua fled the area, winding up at a mission station. Kamani returned home to Kagaita Ridge as a missionary, and Wamaitha was killed by an angry villager who believed her sin was the cause of a drought. Although the youths were to "forge the first link in the chain of the future," it is clear that the tensions of moving into that future age remain unresolved.

Kahiga, Samuel. *The Girl From Abroad*. Nairobi: Heinemann, 1974.

Matthew Mbathia falls in love with his childhood friend June after she returns to Kenya from her studies in the U.S.A. The story moves between Mbathia's job and apartment in Nairobi and his family homestead in semirural Kangemi, highlighting the tensions between generations (especially with Mbathia's conservative Christian father) and the rootlessness of the new professional class of which Mbathia is a member. June, the "girl from abroad," seems to offer the key to resolving these tensions, so her ultimate departure is a disappointing blow to Mbathia.

Kahiga, Samuel. *Lover in the Sky.* Nairobi: Heinemann, 1975. Spear Books.

> As an Air Force pilot, Thuo lives life in the fast lane until he meets the beautiful Seneiya. The mystery surrounding her builds until he finds out about her previous marriage and child. Thuo's plane crash (from which he escapes intact) on the day he finds out only draws the two closer together. Although they do not marry in the end, Seneiya always fondly remembers her "lover in the sky" during the Air Force flyovers at subsequent Independence Day celebrations.

Kahiga, Samuel. *When the Stars Are Scattered.* Nairobi: Longman, 1979.

> Ricky, an engineer working in Northeast Province, takes a day trip to Mombasa, where he runs into Sophie. Their meeting brings up memories of their love affair in years gone by.

Kahiga, Samuel. *Dedan Kimathi: The Real Story.* Nairobi: Longman, 1990.

> An historical novel about the Mau Mau freedom fighter Dedan Kimathi, told from the perspective of Agnes, a woman who joined the fighters and stayed in the Aberdares forest until independence. Kimathi is shown as a tragic figure, and the freedom fighters are seriously divided in their loyalties to the camp of literate leaders under Kimathi and a group of illiterates under Stanley Mathenge.

Kahiga, Samuel. *Paradise Farm*. Nairobi: Longman, 1993.

> When we first meet Joe he has lost his memory and has just stumbled onto Paradise Farm, an oasis in the Kenyan highlands that turns out to be his own farm. The rest of the tale involves the gradual recovery of his memory, and a love story that moves between Kenya and New York City. Also featured are an adoptive grandmother with supernatural powers, a look at the underbelly of New York, and a fanciful ending that attempts to reconcile the characters' material desires with a narrative commitment (on the surface at least) to social justice. The novel won third place in the 1995 Jomo Kenyatta Award for Literature.

Kang'ethe, Karanja wa. *Mission to Gehenna*. Nairobi: Heinemann, 1989.

> In this "Kenyan *Inferno*," Kimuri and Keega are transported mysteriously to Gehenna, the kingdom of Satan Lucifer. It's a world rather more like earth than one might expect. Satan is the dictator in a place where cheating, corruption and killing are commonplace; slums abound, religion is corrupt. There are epidemics (including AIDS) and employment problems, and the politicians are greedy. In short, the village of Ahera (Hades) bears more than a passing resemblance to Nairobi.

Karanja, David. *The Girl Was Mine*. Nairobi: East African Educational Publishers, 1996. Spear Books.

> Douglas Kamau and Nancy Wanja come from very different backgrounds: He is an orphan from an impoverished background, and she the daughter of a millionaire. They fall in love when they meet at the University of Nairobi, but she is seduced by a rich American and

he is jailed for a crime of desperation. In prison, he writes a book about his experiences, *The Girl Was Mine*, which becomes an instant international bestseller—and brings Nancy back to him.

Karauri, Mathew Adams. *The Devil You Know*. Nairobi: Karma Publishing Company, 1996.

Benedict Shaka proves himself to be an honest and principled young man, beginning with his brave opposition to secondary school bullies. At university, he is arrested (then released) for being an activist. Eventually, he enters politics, running for parliament against a corrupt and crafty incumbent. The novel closes with a call for political change.

Karoki, John Njoroge. *The Land Is Ours*. Nairobi: East African Literature Bureau, 1970.

Elijah, an educated Kikuyu, is made a chief by the British authorities just before the outbreak of the Mau Mau Emergency. His loyalty is torn between the colonial powers he serves and the indigenous nationalism represented by Mau Mau. When he opposes the Kiama Kia Muingi, a local resistance group, his son is blinded by them.

Kibera, Leonard. *Voices in the Dark*. Nairobi: East African Publishing House, 1970.

The first true urban novel from Kenya, this story is about the disillusionment of University of Nairobi student and playwright, Gerald Timundu. The narrative highlights the role of multinationals in postindependence Kenya, the marginalization of the Mau Mau fighters, and the ineffectiveness of the university as a site of resistance.

Kimani, John Kiggia. *Life and Times of a Bank Robber*. Nairobi: Heinemann, 1988. Spear Books.

> The first-person, real-life confessional of Kimani's involvement in a bank robbery in Nakuru in 1970, for which he spent 15 years in prison. The story includes an inside account of the deplorable conditions in Kenya's prisons.

Kimani, John Kiggia. *Prison Is Not a Holiday Camp*. Nairobi: East African Educational Publishers, 1994. Spear Books.

> In a tale that is similar to his first novel, Kiggia moves to Nairobi during the Emergency, when he is still a young boy. Growing up without the discipline of family structures, he soon resorts to petty thievery, and eventually bank robbery. After being caught, jailed and eventually released, he is a rehabilitated and repentant man.

Kiriamiti, John. *My Life in Crime*. Nairobi: Heinemann, 1984.

> When John, a.k.a Jack Zollo, leaves Murang'a to go to secondary school in Nairobi, that is the beginning of his undoing. After being expelled he begins his descent into the world of crime, beginning with picking pockets and eventually becoming leader of a gang of bank robbers. The narrator is caught and thrown into Kamiti Prison for 13 years. The story ends on a penitent note that is belied by the celebratory tone throughout and the self-congratulatory style of the sequel.

Kiriamiti, John. *My Life with a Criminal: Milly's Story*. Nairobi: Heinemann, 1989. Spear Books.

> A sequel to *My Life in Crime*, this is the same story, but this time told from the perspective of Zollo's wife, Milly.

Kiriamiti, John. *Son of Fate*. Nairobi: East African Educational Publishers, 1994. Spear Books.

> Adam is the "Son of Fate," a young man struggling to survive by his wits in Nairobi after being released from jail. When even the cheapest lodgings on River Road prove too expensive, he takes to living on the streets and surviving with odd jobs. Eventually, good luck comes his way.

Kitololo, Paul. *Shortcut to Hell*. Nairobi: Newfields Communications, 1983.

> Joe Mamba becomes entangled in a case involving manslaughter and robbery with violence. An exciting police chase finally catches up with him at a coastal resort.

Kiyeng, Stephen. *Echoes of Two Worlds*. Kenya Literature Bureau, 1985.

> The coming-of-age story of Kipsang, a Kalenjin youth. We see all the stages of his life, including hunting expeditions, conflicts with his friends, initiation and courtships. When he returns to his village after an absence, his mother has died. The subsequent death of his uncle also leaves him saddened, facing the world on his own.

Kize, Mary. *Love and Learn*. Nairobi: Transafrica, 1974. Afromance.

> Jeannie, a new sociology student at the university, is fed up with her happy-go-lucky boyfriend, Ricky, who can never get serious. She falls in love with a new professor, who has recently completed studies in America.

Koigi wa Wamwere. *A Woman Reborn.* Nairobi: Heinemann, 1980. Spear Books.

> During the night following the death of the merchant smuggler Kimeria, his wife Njooki is unable to sleep. She mourns his death, but in a long and frank conversation with Wahome she discusses how it in fact means a new freedom for her. The novel was reportedly written on toilet paper while the author was in detention at Kamiti Maximum Security Prison.

Kulet, Henry R. ole. *Is It Possible?* Nairobi: Longman, 1971.

> Lerionka demonstrates that, despite his father's objections, it is possible to integrate Maasai tradition and a modern education: to "hold a spear in one hand, the sticks in the other, and books at the same time." The narrative includes appeals for national unity above tribal allegiance and respect for (but not a blind allegiance to) tradition.

Kulet, Henry R. ole. *To Become a Man.* Nairobi: Longman, 1972.

> When Leshao's father decides to remove him from school, he faces a quandary: he is expected to participate in cattle raids, but he is convinced this is stealing and therefore wrong. Leshao and his friends grow up at a time when traditional expectations are being slowly eroded by contact with the outside world. As in *Is It Possible?*, the overriding moral is that a balance must be found between tradition and modernity.

Kulet, Henry R. ole. *The Hunter*. Nairobi: Longman, 1986.

> Leseiyo, a young Maasai *moran* (warrior), is hired by
> Richmond Sipaya to work as a guide for Elube Safaris
> Limited. When Sipaya's company becomes involved in
> poaching, Leseiyo opposes them, eventually taking the
> law into his own hands and killing Sipaya. The novel
> highlights the conflict between traditional Maasai ways
> of life and beliefs, and the commercial tourist industry.

Kulet, Henry R. ole. *Daughter of Maa*. Nairobi: Longman,
1987.

> Maa village is taken by storm when the new teacher,
> Anna Nalungu, arrives. Although a number of men want
> to marry her, she rebuffs all suitors. In the end, it is the
> communication between two women, Anna and Seleina,
> that breaks down barriers and encourages common un-
> derstanding among the women of the village.

Kulet, Henry R. ole. *Moran No More*. Nairobi: Longman,
1990. Masterpiece series.

> Roiman Ole Mugie moves to Nakuru at the age of nine,
> where he is raised by his uncle in a multitribal setting.
> The story focuses on the choices Roiman makes as he
> gradually discards specific markers and traditions of his
> heritage: clothes, circumcision, and so forth. However,
> the corrupt financier Za-Kale represents the dangers of
> completely abandoning traditional morality.

Kyendo, Muli wa. *Whispers*. Nairobi: Longman, 1975.

> Josephine moves to Nairobi from Machakos when she
> can no longer get along with her stepmother. The city
> life, she discovers, is especially difficult for a single

woman. She is fired from her secretarial job for refusing her boss's sexual advances. She realizes too late that she should have married Musyoki instead of the rich but uncaring Joseph.

Kyendo, Muli wa. *The Surface Beneath.* Nairobi: Longman, 1981.

A Kenyan student goes to Berlin to study African literature. The story focuses on the alienation and disillusionment of studying in a foreign land.

Likimani, Muthoni Gachanja. *They Shall Be Chastised.* Nairobi: East African Literature Bureau, 1974.

An account of the influence of missionaries on traditional life in Kenya. The author, the daughter of one of Kenya's first Anglican ministers, presents an account of both the advantages of mission activity as well as the social disruption they cause.

Likimani, Muthoni Gachanja. *What Does a Man Want?* Nairobi: East African Literature Bureau, 1974.

This novel in verse form explores the difficulties of living with an unfaithful man in a modern urban setting.

Lusweti, Bramwell. *The Way to the Town Hall.* London: Macmillan, 1984.

Political struggle in rural Nababa town ensues after the unnatural death of the town councillor, Mpole Wanyonyi. Self-interest and deceit are present at all levels of community life.

Macgoye, Marjorie Oludhe. *Murder in Majengo*. Nairobi: Oxford University Press, 1972.

> When prominent lawyer Obonyo is murdered in the Majengo slums of a Western Kenyan town (probably Kisumu), the investigation uncovers all manner of interesting connections. Political opposition leaders Wasere and Rapar, schoolgirl Lois Akinyi, Fatima the brothel owner, and the English schoolteacher Vera Willett find their lives entwined in a complex web of political intrigue and economic self-preservation. More than merely a tightly woven murder story, Macgoye's first novel is remarkable for its analysis of urban Luo society in postindependence Kenya. The richly textured female characters in particular are forerunners of the women in Macgoye's later texts.

Macgoye, Marjorie Oludhe. *Coming to Birth*. Nairobi: Heinemann, 1986.

> A young and naive Paulina arrives in Nairobi at the same time that Operation Anvil, the crackdown against Mau Mau by the colonial authorities, is at its height. There are three births in this story: the birth of the Kenya as a nation, the birth of Paulina as a mature woman, and the imminent birth of her child.

Macgoye, Marjorie Oludhe. *The Present Moment*. Nairobi: Heinemann, 1987.

> Thirty women live in a home for the destitute elderly in Eastleigh (called "the Refuge"), under the care of the Matron and a number of young nurses. Their stories are interwoven in this novel, as is the history of Kenya as a nation.

Macgoye, Marjorie Oludhe. *Street Life*. Nairobi: Heinemann, 1987.

> A series of connected vignettes bring us the stories of a variety of people who pass through Nairobi's streets: Simon Oluoch, an amputee; Mwangi wa Vitabu, the used book seller; Jack the Black, a shoeshine; Almasi Kassam, a playboy and advertising salesman; and others.

Macgoye, Marjorie Oludhe. *Victoria and Murder in Majengo*. London: Macmillan, 1993.

> *Victoria*, the "prequel" to *Murder in Majengo* (re-published in the same volume), tells the story of Lois Akinyi's mother, Victoria Abiero, a successful prostitute-cum-businesswoman.

Macgoye, Marjorie Oludhe. *Homing In*. Nairobi: East African Educational Publishers, 1994.

> Ellen Smith is the elderly widow of a Rift Valley farmer, living with a caretaker/servant, Martha Kimani. Flashbacks and reminiscences by both women reconstruct their interlinked lives, families and society.

Macgoye, Marjorie Oludhe. *Chira*. Nairobi: East African Educational Publishers, 1997.

> Otieno, a messenger in a Nairobi office, helps rescue the political and business prospects of his employer through some clever sleuthing. *Chira*, the Luo term for a "wasting disease" that is also used for AIDS, is the structuring metaphor for Kenyan society.

Macharia, David. *The Smasher*. Nairobi: Kenya Literature Bureau, 1984.

Set among the ridges of Kikuyu territory in an unspecified precolonial era, this is the story of Mumero, a *muhoi* (outsider) who divides the community by preaching a new set of Utopian religious beliefs. In particular, Mumero's brand of religion opposes traditional ancestor worship. In the end, Mumero and his followers are discredited, the people return to their traditional religious practices, and Gatarwa is given the title of "the Smasher" because of his strong opposition to Mumero's heresy.

Maillu, David. *My Dear Bottle*. Nairobi: Comb Books, 1973.

The musings of a drunkard trying to forget about his problems. Told in blank verse.

Maillu, David. *Unfit for Human Consumption*. Nairobi: Comb Books, 1973.

In Maillu's first novel, which started his long publishing career, civil servant Jonathan Kinama cannot control his desire for sex and alcohol. He eventually commits suicide.

Maillu, David. *After 4:30*. Nairobi: Comb Books, 1974. (Reprinted in a revised version by Maillu Publishing House, 1987.)

Perhaps Maillu's most widely read book, *After 4:30* is also one that helped earn him a reputation as a "pornographic" writer. This is a long prose poem in the style of Okot p'Bitek that centers on relationships between bosses and secretaries after working hours. Several central characters emerge: Emili Katango, who is a poor prostitute; her friend Lili, an attractive secretary who doesn't manage to evade the amorous advances of her boss; and other boyfriends, wives, and acquaintances.

Maillu, David. *Kadosa*. Nairobi: David Maillu Publishers, 1975.

> The bizarre and unsettling story of Kadosa, an extrater-restrial, supernatural female who radically interrupts the life of John Mutava, a recent recipient of a doctoral degree in philosophy who is studying the occult.

Maillu, David. *Dear Daughter*. Nairobi: Comb Books, 1976.

> A father disinherits his daughter for what he considers her loose morals. She defends her out-of-wedlock preg-nancy in her own letter, and her mother puts in a good word for her.

Maillu, David. *Dear Monika*. Nairobi: Comb Books, 1976.

> Joana Mwaka writes to his wife Monika, apologizing for the way he has treated her and begging her to return to him.

Maillu, David. *No!* Nairobi: Comb Books, 1976.

> Washington Ndava is a senior civil servant who takes advantage of his position to seduce the wife of one of his junior workers. When his own wife deserts him, Ndava tries various methods of committing suicide. Eventually he succeeds by driving his car into a build-ing.

Maillu, David. *The Equatorial Assignment*. London: Macmillan, 1980. Pacesetters.

> This is the original Benni Kamba adventure, in which our hero infiltrates an organization that is trying to as-sume control of the African continent by placing pup-

pet presidents in every country. Kamba is agent 009 for the National Integrity Service of Africa (NISA).

Maillu, David. *For Mbatha and Rabeka*. London: Macmillan, 1980. Pacesetters.

> Mbatha and Rabeka's childhood friendship blossoms into love, despite opposition from various quarters. But when Rabeka is taken to Nairobi, she becomes dissatisfied with the limitations of her prospects and decides to marry the wealthy Mawa. In the end, she realizes the foolishness of her materialistic desires.

Maillu, David. *The Ayah*. Nairobi: Heinemann, 1986. Spear Books.

> Beatrice Kavele, a young girl from Machakos, goes to Nairobi to work for the Makumbi family in their Harambee Estates house, leaving behind her boyfriend and her impoverished family. In Nairobi, her new employers exploit her, and after she is discovered to be pregnant (by Mr. Makumbi), she is thrown out of the house and loses her newborn child to stray dogs. She returns to the countryside to begin the healing process.

Maillu, David. *Benni Kamba 009 in Operation DXT*. Nairobi: Heinemann, 1986. Spear Books.

> Special agent Benni Kamba is assigned to blow up a factory that is producing the deadly chemical DXT from its base on a Mediterranean island.

Maillu, David. *Untouchable*. Nairobi: Maillu Publishing House, 1987.

An interracial love story, as university students Tochi (an Indian) and Moses (a Kamba) begin a romantic relationship that is disapproved of by both families.

Maillu, David. *Thorns of Life*. London: Macmillan, 1988. Pacesetters.

Silvesta Maweu works in Mombasa, two hundred miles away from his rural Machakos home, leaving his beautiful new wife Nzivele open to the seducing wiles of other men—especially the rich and handsome Simon Mosi. His aging mother tries to keep Nzivele on the straight and narrow, and the marriage intact.

Maillu, David. *My Dear Mariana/Kumya Ivu*. Nairobi: Maillu Publishing House, 1989.

Mariana gets a scholarship to study in the U.S., but her boyfriend tries to talk her out of it. She still wants to go, until she discovers she is pregnant. The pastor has the last word, urging her not to have an abortion and to save her studies for later in life. Parallel texts in English and in Kamba.

Maillu, David. *Without Kiinua Mgongo*. Nairobi: Maillu Publishing House, 1989.

Written in a variety of *sheng*, the mixture of Swahili and English typically heard on the streets of Nairobi, this is the story of a millionaire's corrupt family and their faithful servants. Katherine Mbuta, the daughter, becomes pregnant and blames it on Nzuki, the son of the servant Mwangangi. Mr. Mbuta, realizing that his ugly and unintelligent daughter is not likely to find another husband, convinces Nzuki to marry her, even without a brideprice. Since he is an intelligent boy, Nzuki soon becomes closely involved in Mbuta's business dealings and is ready to inherit the family fortune. In the end, Katherine and Nzuki discover true love for each other.

Maillu, David. *Broken Drum*. Nairobi: Jomo Kenyatta Publishers and Maillu Publishing House, 1991.

This 1100-page volume attempts an epic look at 200 years of Kamba history, beginning with Nzie (born 1770), his son Nzimba (1860), grandson Ngomo (1900), and great-grandson Ngewa (1930). Most of the action is set in postindependence Nairobi, centering on the conflict between Bonifas Ngewa and his wife Vikirose. The latter is fascinated with anything modern and scorns traditional life, while Bonifas is obsessed with returning to his roots and rediscovering his past. Much of the text involves the narrator's philosophical musing, put in the mouths of various characters and covering topics Maillu has written about elsewhere: polygamy, religion, international aid, traditional cultural practices, and national development.

Maillu, David. *P.O. Box I Love You, Via My Heart*. Nairobi: Maillu Publishing House, 1991.

When Philip Ndimu goes to study in Sweden, he falls in love with Sonya, but fails to tell her that he already has a wife in Kenya. Two years after Philip returns to Kenya, Sonya discovers the truth and—still in love with him—goes to Kenya to confront him.

Mak'Oloo, Omondi. *Too Young to Die*. London: Macmillan, 1986. Pacesetters.

Melle and Zania are criminal agents for the Vulture, the "brains behind Africa's biggest crime network." They are sent to Nairobi to steal the Dabu, a priceless stone owned by a Maasai trading tycoon.

Mak'Oloo, Omondi. *Times Beyond.* Nairobi: Heinemann, 1991. Spear Books.

Waweru Njuhia is a Kenyan student in Hungary, where—in addition to studying—he indulges his hobbies of boxing and sex.

Malimoto, P. (P.G. Okoth). *Bless the Wicked.* Nairobi: Foundation Books, 1973.

Malimoto, a character from Okoth's *Drum* magazine columns, muses on the problems of modern Kenya: sugar daddies, pollution, politics, and other topics.

Mangua, Charles. *Son of Woman.* Nairobi: East African Publishing House, 1971. Modern African Library.

Mangua's antihero, Dodge Kiunyu, manages to graduate from Makerere and attain a civil service job despite his low-brow beginnings as the son of an Eastleigh prostitute. But he soon tires of the routine and becomes involved in a tax evasion scheme that backfires, landing Kiunyu in jail. In the end, he marries his childhood friend and fellow criminal Tonia, and they settle down in Mombasa with the promise to reform their lives.

Mangua, Charles. *A Tail in the Mouth.* Nairobi: East African Publishing House, 1972.

Samson Moira's numerous career changes provide an insight into a variety of facets of Kenyan society. At various points he is a priest in training, a home-guard turned forest fighter for the Mau Mau, a taxi-driver, and a happy-go-lucky drunkard. In the end he decides to leave the city, which he realizes has been "sucking my blood," and return to the land.

Mangua, Charles. *Son of Woman in Mombasa*. Nairobi: Heinemann, 1986. Spear Books.

Taking up where *Son of Woman* left off, we find that Dodge Kiunyu and Tonia are living in Mombasa, where they are not surprisingly having a hard time getting along. Kiunyu becomes embroiled in a money laundering scheme with foreign ships that dock in Mombasa. When he double-crosses his partners he finds himself on the run from them and from the law.

Mangua, Charles. *Kanina and I*. Nairobi: East African Educational Publishers, 1994. Spear Books.

Kanina and Njeru are orphaned when their parents are killed by a white settler farmer during the Mau Mau Emergency. Kanina eventually joins the freedom fighters in the forest, but Njeru becomes a member of the police, hunting the Mau Mau. After various adventures, the two are reunited in the end.

Mathenge wa Ndirangu. *High Hopes*. Nairobi: Mathenge wa Ndirangu, 1994.

A presidential candidate, known only as "the Green Belt," launches his campaign on bicycle, bus and matatu. His down-to-earth campaign, his honesty, and his penchant for story-telling capture the hearts of the voters.

Mazrui, Ali. *The Trial of Christopher Okigbo*. Nairobi: Heinemann, 1971.

Christopher Okigbo was a Nigerian poet who was killed while fighting for Biafran independence in the Nigerian civil war. Mazrui imagines him on trial for putting regional and ethnic allegiances ahead of pan-Africanism.

Mbugua, Johnson. *Mumbi's Brideprice*. Nairobi: Longman, 1971.

Mwai is in love with Mumbi but unsure if her family will accept his marriage proposal. His hopes are dashed when her father demands an unusually high brideprice. He solves the problem by leading a successful raid against the Maasai, capturing large numbers of cattle and assuring his marriage to Mumbi.

M'Imanyara, Alfred Mwyti. *Agony on a Hide*. Nairobi: East African Publishing House, 1973.

Three generations of two families from "Mugweland" (in rural Meru) have to adapt to the changes that history brings. Mutema, a village leader, has to face the military defeat of his community by invading "ghosts"—the colonial forces. His children move to Nairobi, where they also find it difficult to make the necessary adjustments. Throughout the story, Mutema's daughter Wanja feels a continuous "strange call": to return to Fig Tree Village, her home.

Mote, Jasinta. *The Flesh*. Nairobi: Comb Books, 1975.

"Produced" by David Maillu. The first-hand and personal account of the life of a Nairobi prostitute named Jasinta Mote. Told in blank verse.

Mude, Mude Dae. *The Hills Are Falling*. Nairobi: Transafrica, 1979.

Galge, a young man from a large Gabra family, is among the first from Marsabit to have an opportunity to go to secondary school. Galge becomes an educated and eventually urbanized young man, and the primary conflict that emerges has to do with the expectations of his family. Eventually Galge realizes that he will have to drop some of his personal goals in order to answer the higher obligations to his family.

Mudida, Francis. *The Bottle Friends*. Nairobi: Kenya Literature Bureau, 1980.

Aniluga reviews his life after being put in prison for drunk driving. He repents the excesses of his drinking habits, his superficial friends, and his frequent visits to prostitutes.

Mugot, Hazel. *Black Night of Quiloa*. Nairobi: East African Publishing House, 1971.

Hima drops her plans to marry Abu when a white stranger comes to town and sweeps her off her feet. They go to England, where he betrays her; she finds the city dehumanizing and cold. In the end, she returns to search for healing in her home at Quiloa.

Mulwa, David. *Master and Servant*. Nairobi: Longman, 1979.

Young Kituku develops a close relationship with Hamad, a house-servant whose mysterious past is never fully uncovered. We learn something of the tragedy of his life, however, and the love he has for Eileen, his master's wife.

Mumba, Maurice Kambishera. *The Wrath of Koma*. Nairobi: Heinemann, 1987.

Set among the Mijikenda during colonial times, this is a warning to those who forsake traditional values. Old Chembe attempts to cure his son's madness, which was caused by his lack of gratefulness in the first place. But he takes shortcuts, further enraging the ancestral spirits.

Muruah, George Kamau. *Never Forgive Father*. Nairobi: East African Literature Bureau, 1972.

An exploration of the moral dilemmas of city life. Kariuki meets the girl he caused to go into prostitution, and in trying to make amends he ruins his marriage. In the end he kills himself while trying to drive away from the scene of a crime.

Mutahi, Wahome. *Three Days on the Cross*. Nairobi: Heinemann, 1991. Kenya Writers Series.

Albert Momodu, a bank director, and Ogundipe Chipota, a journalist, are wrongly implicated as members of the July 10 Movement, a group committed to the overthrow of the Illustrious One, the dictator in a nameless country that bears an uncanny resemblance to Kenya of the 1980s. The two are arrested, tortured for three days and left for hyenas, in a manner similar to the fate of Kenyan politician J.M. Kariuki. The text was in fact prophetic of Mutahi's own detention, and he revised it for publication following his release.

Mutahi, Wahome. *The Jail Bugs*. Nairobi: Longman, 1992.

Albert Kweyu's accidental killing of a child with his car one Sunday morning leads to his 10-month detention in Wakora Wengi ("many thugs") prison. This is the story of his prison experience, featuring regular beatings, inedible food, lice, and insanitary conditions. Though a morbid tale, it is told with a wry humor. The story is based on Mutahi's own 15-month experience in prison. It was Kenya's only nomination for the Commonwealth Prize for Literature in 1993.

Mutiso, Muli. *Sugar Babies*. Nairobi: Transafrica, 1975.

The "Benz Man" goes from one sexual conquest to another, using his position as a senior executive in a Nairobi company as leverage. A popular novel set in blank verse.

Mwanga, Abel. *Nyangeta: The Name from the Calabash*. Nairobi: East African Literature Bureau, 1976.

Set in rural Western Kenya, the story of the birth and upbringing of Nyangeta includes and explains many of the customs of the Ebukwaya. Nyangeta eventually marries Busa. Meanwhile, there are occasional signs of increasing conflict with Europeans, particularly over taxes.

Mwangi, Crispin E. *The Secret of the Waterfall*. Nairobi: East African Publishing House, 1977.

Two young men—an American and a Maasai—accidentally uncover a drug-smuggling racket. Their sleuthing eventually leads to assisting the police in an exciting chase and arrest sequence.

Mwangi, Crispin E. *The Operator*. Nairobi: Heinemann, 1989. Spear Books.

Diana's religious but distant father and an unstructured family life turn her into a naughty high school student who eventually becomes a prostitute, first in Nairobi and then Mombasa. She begins to realize that she is in a dangerous line of work when her friend Nancy dies in a botched abortion. In the end she leaves the city, determined to return to her rural roots and settle down.

Mwangi, Meja. *Kill Me Quick*. Nairobi: Heinemann, 1973.

Meja and Maina are young boys trying to eke out a living on the streets of Nairobi. The novel is a picaresque but ultimately tragic account of their failure to find employment and their gradual involvement in a life of crime.

Mwangi, Meja. *Carcase for Hounds*. Nairobi: Heinemann, 1974.

A Mau Mau novel focusing on the conflict between General Haraka, a former village chief, and the British troops led by Captain Kingsley. In the end Haraka is killed along with his lieutenant, Kimamo.

Mwangi, Meja. *Taste of Death*. Nairobi: East African Publishing House, 1975.

The General and his sidekick Kariuki are pitted against the white Inspector Cowdrey in this Mau Mau tale. When the General dies, the cohesion of the freedom fighters is lost.

Mwangi, Meja. *Going Down River Road*. Nairobi: Heinemann, 1976.

Ben, a Nairobi construction worker whose low-paying job is always precarious, lives in squalor and frequents the River Road bars. His life becomes complicated when his girlfriend Wini deserts him, leaving him alone to care for Baby.

Mwangi, Meja. *The Bushtrackers*. Nairobi: Longman, 1979.

John Kimathi and Frank Burkell team up as game rangers who set out to foil Al Haji's poaching operation. This is the book version of an original screenplay cowritten with the American journalist Gary Strieker.

Mwangi, Meja. *The Cockroach Dance*. Nairobi: Longman, 1979.

Dusman Gonzaga lives in Dacca House, a dilapidated set of apartments on Nairobi's Grogan Road. Like Ben in *Going Down River Road*, his life is a downward spiral of underemployment and miserable living conditions. In attempting to better his own life, he realizes that he needs to take more seriously the rest of the "faceless masses"—for whom the cockroaches are a metaphor—who share his plight.

Mwangi, Meja. *Bread of Sorrow*. Nairobi: Longman, 1987.

Diamond smuggling and gun running feature in this action-packed story that moves from London to Johannesburg to Mozambique to Nanyuki and finally to the small island of Msimbati, off Tanzania's coast.

Mwangi, Meja. *The Return of Shaka*. Nairobi: Longman, 1989.

Moshesh, having studied in the U.S. for a number of years, is finally convinced to return home to Ezuluni, but plans to do so with a sufficient armed force to liberate his homeland and build a new African nation. Things don't work out quite as planned, but in the process we get a look at the "River Road" areas of North America—

the Greyhound bus routes—and the African student community in the U.S.

Mwangi, Meja. *Weapon of Hunger*. Nairobi: Longman, 1989.

A novel in the tradition of Mwangi's adventure tales, rather than his urban trilogy, the setting is this time the fictional nation of Borku, which is experiencing drought and famine, exacerbated by civil war. Jack Rivers, an American rock star organizes a crew of unemployed musicians to deliver a convoy of food through the desert, spurning government resistance and scorning the rebels and bandits.

Mwangi, Meja. *Striving for the Wind*. Nairobi: Heinemann, 1990.

Although more in the style and spirit of his critical urban novels than his adventure thrillers, this story is set entirely in rural central Kenya. The main conflict is over land control. The wealthy and influential landowner Baba Pesa wants to buy up the final plot of land in the area, which is owned by his worker Baba Baru. Colorful character sketches, lively bar scenes, and Mwangi's typical wry humor fill the novel.

Mwaura, Joshua. *The Sky Is the Limit*. Nairobi: East African Literature Bureau, 1974.

A story of intergenerational conflict. Ngarachu has a difficult time dealing with the changes in his village, but his son Mwangi manages to become a cabinet minister in the new national government. The sky is the limit to his ambitions.

Mwaura, Joshua. *He Man*. Nairobi: East African Literature Bureau, 1977.

> The adventures of Kuria lead him through all the typical urban problems. Money and sex corrupt him completely. He begins to rethink his life when he barely escapes death after Palestinian terrorists hijack an airplane taking Kuria to Sweden. The plane is blown up, and his fortune with it.

Mwaura, Joshua. *The Price of Sin*. Nairobi: Kenya Literature Bureau, 1982.

> Roland Macharia is unhappy despite his family and job. His former life catches up with him as he realizes he has to pay the price for past transgressions. In the end, a priest helps him understand his sins and how to relieve this burden.

Mwaura, Mike. *The Renegade*. Nairobi: East African Literature Bureau, 1972.

> Kunjuga fails to meet his father's expectations after getting an education. Kunjuga neglects his family shamelessly. As a result, he father is left destitute and lonely in his old age.

Mwebesa, Mike. *Encounter*. Nairobi: Uzima Press, 1979.

> An autobiographical account of how an encounter with Christianity transformed a drunkard into a new man.

Mwiwawi, Andrew M. *The Act*. Nairobi: Comb Books, 1976.

> Menza is tormented by his wife's infidelity. His patience finally runs out, and he murders her lover.

Namale, Ambayisi. *Honourable Criminals.* Nairobi: East African Educational Publishers, 1994.

> When the Kenyan president announces that he is dissolving parliament and calling new elections, Richard Okumu decides to run against his old nemesis, Apanja Muremula, in Kakamega's Ingwe constituency. In this contest between "honourable criminals," Okumu comes out the loser.

Ndii, Ayub. *A Brief Assignment.* Nairobi: Heinemann, 1976. Spear Books.

> The adventures of the Mooday Gang include living by their wits and breaking into wealthy Nairobi houses. Their fast living eventually catches up with them, and Jip, the protagonist, commits suicide.

Ndii, Ayub. *Colour of Carnations.* Nairobi: East African Educational Publishers, 1994. Spear Books.

> Roger dumps his girlfriend Joelene after he meets her cousin Libby. From then on, it's a tempestuous love relationship, as Roger and Libby's independent personalities are frequently at cross purposes. Things get even worse after their marriage.

Ndissio-Otieno, Moses. *A Blurring Horizon.* Nairobi: Ndissio-Otieno, 1991.

> Ochieng is given a high-ranking job in a large corporation in Nairobi, and the ensuing plot centers on power struggles within the company, Ochieng's relationship with his girlfriend Lilly, and the funeral for Ochieng following his murder by hired thugs. A creative and introspective novel that needs only a good editor. High-

lighted are urban-rural conflicts, the interplay of modern and traditional lifestyles, religious syncretism, and education.

Ng'ang'a, Daniel Simonson. *Young Today, Old Tomorrow.* Nairobi: Njogu Gitene Publications, 1971.

Muturi is a veteran of World War II, having fought for the British in East Asia. His return to Kenya is difficult, however; he feels cut off from his community and goes to Nairobi to look for work. Muturi assists the police in arresting Murenga, who had married and then abandoned his sister. The book's Introduction by then-Vice President Daniel arap Moi praises Kenya's writers, particularly those who demonstrate the moral that "the long arm of the law remains active at all times."

Ngubiah, Stephen N. *A Curse from God.* Nairobi: East African Literature Bureau, 1970.

This story, set in fictional Karagu, emphasizes the conflict between traditional Kikuyu practices and new, Christian ways. Karagu is cursed with a variety of problems, including a severe famine.

Ngugi wa Thiong'o. *Weep Not, Child.* London: Heinemann, 1964.
Njoroge is a young Kikuyu boy growing up during the Emergency. His hopes of getting an education are dashed when his father is arrested as a Mau Mau suspect. This was the first published novel in English by an East African writer.

Ngugi wa Thiong'o. *The River Between.* Nairobi: Heinemann, 1965.

Ngugi's first novel (although published second) focuses on the conflicts between Christianity and Kikuyu tradition in rural preindependence Kenya. Waiyaki and Nyambura are separated by their families' differing beliefs, symbolized by the River Honia running between their respective ridges.

Ngugi wa Thiong'o. *A Grain of Wheat*. Nairobi: Heinemann, 1967.

The novel explores the moment of Kenya's independence, including complex questions of complicity and betrayal in the independence struggle. Mugo is considered a village hero and is asked to give the speech during the local Uhuru celebrations. Although people consider him modest for declining the opportunity, it turns out that he had betrayed an important Mau Mau leader.

Ngugi wa Thiong'o. *Petals of Blood*. London: Heinemann, 1977. Reprinted by Dutton (New York, 1978).

In a series of flashbacks used to gain insight on the murders of three Kenyan businessmen in the town of Ilmorog, the novel criticizes the corrupt direction of postcolonial Kenyan society and calls for unified resistance by peasants and workers.

Ngugi wa Thiong'o. *Devil on the Cross*. Nairobi: Heinemann, 1982.

Ngugi's own translation of his Kikuyu novel, *Ciaitani Mutharaba-ini* (1980; originally written on toilet paper while in Kamiti Prison). Wariinga goes from despair and thoughts of suicide to a new consciousness and determination to fight the injustices in Kenyan society.

Ngugi wa Thiong'o. *Matigari*. Nairobi: Heinemann, 1989.

A translation by Wangui wa Goro of Ngugi's Kikuyu novel, *Matigari ma Njiruungi* (1987). The legendary figure of the Mau Mau fighter Matigari returns from the forests to take up a new struggle against neocolonial oppression in Kenya.

Ngumy, James. *Poisoned Bait*. London: Macmillan, 1992. Pacesetters.

Wanja's love for her school-age boyfriend Victor is in trouble when a local landowner begins to pursue her. Wanja's father goes into debt, and the landowner claims Wanja's hand in marriage as payment. Things come to a head at a climactic village meeting headed by a wise chief.

Ngurukie, Pat Wambui. *I Will Be Your Substitute*. Nairobi: Kenya Literature Bureau, 1984.

In this story of the triumph of love over ethnic separatism, Carol Nyokabi (a Kikuyu from Karatina) eventually marries Sanjay Patel (an Asian living in Nairobi). Along the way she is wooed by Njoroge and by Philip Maina, the latter promising that "I will be your substitute" if her love for Sanjay should ever fail. Carol becomes the owner of a clothing store on Nairobi's Biashara Street.

Ngurukie, Pat Wambui. *Soldier's Wife*. London: Macmillan, 1989. M Novels.

Pam Kanini marries Jim Mutisya, a soldier in the Kenyan army who is posted to Rhodesia as part of a U.N. peacekeeping force. However, once she is there she quickly realizes that he is violent and unfaithful. She leaves him for a Nigerian.

Ngurukie, Pat Wambui. *Businessman's Wife*. Nairobi: P.W. Ngurukie, 1991.

Jimmy Njuguna, a successful Nairobi businessman, separates from his wife Flora Njoki after she takes to drink and fails to heed the doctor's advice to treat her barrenness. She refuses to grant Jimmy a divorce, making a Christian remarriage impossible for him. So when Flora is found strangled in her bathroom, Jimmy is the obvious suspect.

Ngurukie, Pat Wambui. *Tough Choices*. London: MacMillan, 1991. M Novels.

This moralistic potboiler centers on the conflict between Florence Mwangi and her children when she decides to remarry. Eventually, the children accept Florence's choice while she, in turn, accepts her daughter Wangui's marriage to Wallace.

Nguya, Lydia Mumbi. *The First Seed*. Nairobi: East African Literature Bureau, 1975. (Reprinted by the Kenya Literature Bureau, 1978.)

Set in a precolonial Kikuyu community, this is the story of Kigaruri, an iconoclast who is part Maasai. The story's central conflict is between the Kikuyu and the Maitha-Maasai, who stage a daring and successful cattle raid; Kigaruri leads an equally successful retaliatory raid. However, Kigaruri engages in a number of inappropriate activities: He removes a body from his *shamba* (farm plot) before reaching the age of circumcision, he eats meat that had been sacrificed to the gods, and he perpetuates the family name by adopting the young man that his daughter marries as his own son. Kigaruri is the "first seed" in resisting tradition and defining new social norms.

Ng'weno, Hilary. *The Men from Pretoria*. Nairobi: Longman, 1975.

In this thriller, a South African political defector on the run arrives in Kenya. The journalist "Scoop" Nelson becomes involved.

Njau, Rebeka. *Ripples in the Pool*. Nairobi: Transafrica, 1975. (Reprinted by Heinemann, 1978.)

Gikere brings the prostitute Selina back to the village to be his wife, where she tries to leave behind the sick urban society that she had come to know. The story ends ambiguously, with a murder near the enigmatic pool that is guarded by an old man. He, like the pool, represents the secrets of the land.

Njue, Pal N. *My Lovely Mother*. Nairobi: Comb Books, 1976.

Cento reads his father's diaries in an attempt to understand his mother's death. Told in blank verse.

Nyarango, Peter. *Sunset in Africa: Childhood Memories*. Nairobi: East African Educational Publishers, 1994.

An autobiographical tale about growing up in a Kisii community in the 1950s and 1960s. The high-spirited narrator's tale ends as he is graduating from secondary school.

Nyasani, Joseph and Edward Oyugi. *The Club on the Hill.* Nairobi: Kenya Literature Bureau, 1983.

> The story emphasizes the social differences in the city between those in the former "African locations" and the suburban houses on the hill, as well as the postcolonial reality of a new Kenyan elite in cahoots with European and Japanese capitalists. The story closes with the investigation into the murder of the Norwegian Klaus Juergen.

Obondo-Okoyo, Tom. *A Thorn in the Flesh.* East African Publishing House, 1975. Heartbeat books.

> Peter Bolo takes over the running of Pala Full Primary School when the headmaster is hospitalized and soon becomes a "thorn in the flesh" of all the teachers. Bolo is convinced that he will prove his superiority despite his lack of advanced degrees.

Odaga, Asenath. *Between the Years.* Kisumu: Lake Publishers, 1987.

> When Apon Jaoko returns to Kenya from his studies in England, he discovers that his job with Mpato Incorporated in Nairobi does not pay well enough to meet the expectations of his family and his own desires. He begins to deal in ivory smuggling and other illicit trade, but as he becomes richer his personal problems mount.

Odaga, Asenath. *A Bridge in Time.* Kisumu: Lake Publishers and Enterprises, 1987.

> Thoro is the son of the chief of Mumbo Island, but his life is riddled with problems, including the death of his mother and a love affair with his father's youngest wife.

The action occurs in a precolonial setting, into which Europeans are beginning to appear by the novel's close.

Odaga, Asenath. *Riana*. Kisumu: Lake Publishers and Enterprises, 1991.

Riana is a Luo woman who has had an uphill struggle in life as she fought for her rights and dignity as an independent woman. Looking back on her life, she regrets dropping out of school after standard six in order to marry. Her husband Dhimu, who works at a Malindi hotel, has married a German woman, but the co-wives are unaware of each other's existence. When Dhimu and Ulla die in a plane crash, Riana refuses to be inherited by any of his relatives as custom allows. She marries Sam, who also takes another wife, causing Riana to leave him. In the end, she is influential in organizing a women's group in the community.

Odaga, Asenath. *Endless Road*. Kisumu: Lake Publishers and Enterprises, 1995.

The relationship between Dino and Salmarie is stormy, from their initial meeting, through their courtship, and even in their marriage. They each campaign for political office, running with different parties. Salmarie wins her election, Dino loses his, and in the end they are reconciled.

Ogot, David. *Mission to Uganda*. Nairobi: Designbook Anyange Publications, 1981.

Okello and his friends are involved in adventures in lawless, Idi Amin-era Uganda. They barely make it out alive.

Ogot, Grace. *Promised Land.* Nairobi: East African Publishing House, 1966.

This story of a family who emigrates to Tanganyika highlights the social tensions of life in rural Western Kenya. Nyapol opposes her husband's desire to uproot his family, but she goes along with him, only to see the family fall into disgrace and ruin when he is cursed by an antagonistic neighbor and falls ill.

Ogot, Grace. *The Graduate.* Nairobi: Uzima Press, 1980.

The story of a graduate who goes to America, but who discovers upon returning to Kenya that that things have changed considerably.

Ogot, Grace. *The Strange Bride.* Nairobi: Heinemann, 1989.

First published in Luo as *Miaha* (1983), this novel interprets a Luo myth about the people of Got Awaga, whose peaceful life is interrupted by the sudden appearance of the glamorous but mysterious Nyawir.

Okello, C. *The Prophet.* Nairobi: Uzima Press, 1978.

Set in the fictional country of Mashariki, this is the story of one man's struggle to speak the truth even at great personal cost. As a pastor, Daniel Lanebi initially believes that Christians have no right to speak out about political matters. But as ethnic tensions in the country rise, and after witnessing a brutal execution, Lanebi becomes a prophetic voice for justice.

Olela, Henry and Mary Jane Neuendorffer. *Beyond Those Hills*. London: Evans Brothers, 1966.

> Juma, a Luo boy from Rusinga Island, aims to see more of the world. Education (despite opposition from some family members) is his ticket. The story is filled with anecdotes about growing up: fishing, farming, looking after cows, football matches, the death of the grandfather, dances, and weddings. At book's end, Juma is about to leave for secondary school. Olela, at the time of writing, was a university student in the U.S., and Neuendorffer assisted him; Tom Mboya wrote the Foreword.

Onyango-Abuje, J.C. *Fire and Vengeance*. Nairobi: East African Publishing House, 1975.

> This tale, set in precolonial Luo territory, features Ojuok, an unusual from the start, since he spoke, excreted, and urinated within hours of his birth. The rest of his life is also remarkable for its bizarre events. He becomes a witchdoctor and a night runner and eventually kills his father. In the end, he is convicted in a village ordeal and drowned.

Owino, Henry. *A Man of Two Faces*. Nairobi: Kenya Literature Bureau, 1978.

> Okure has studied abroad, and when he returns to Kenya after a six-year absence, he chooses to reject his family and his girlfriend. Eventually he is jailed, a victim of personal and cultural conflict.

Owino, Rosemary. *Sugar Daddy's Lover*. Nairobi: Heinemann, 1975. Spear Books.

Eighteen-year-old Aggie marries Abed, a rich man of 40. The first months of marriage are fine, but things quickly deteriorate after that. He begins a series of affairs, and Aggie takes up with her old boyfriend Tony. Only after Tony dies, and Aggie's mother and aunt advise her to stick with her husband, does she decide to settle down and to make Abed love her again by becoming a model wife.

Rajab, Hammie. *Rest in Peace, Dear Mother*. Nairobi: Kenya Literature Bureau, 1982.

James's mother, Veronica Mbaga, died only seven years after her marriage to Ruben Waba. It is only on his own wedding night that James learns the truth of the matter from his grandmother. His father, who had a notorious temper, had killed his mother in anger. Set in colonial-era Mombasa.

Ruheni, Mwangi. *What a Life!* Nairobi: Longman, 1972.

Willie works as a hydroelectric technician but still has trouble making ends meet. His well-intentioned plans at budgeting never seem to work out. He gets a boost in income after studying in England, but on returning to Nairobi realizes that it is still difficult to live in the style to which he aspires.

Ruheni, Mwangi. *The Future Leaders*. Nairobi: Heinemann, 1973.

Reuben Ruoro, a Makerere University graduate, is a miserable failure in his first civil service position in precolonial East Africa. After a stint as a teacher he gets another chance with the civil service when independence comes.

Ruheni, Mwangi. *What a Husband!* Nairobi: Longman, 1974.

> Dennis Kinyua, a young executive, has the typical urban problems: marital troubles, difficult mistresses, and involvement in a gem-smuggling conspiracy. In contrast to the corruption of urban society is an idyllic village in a remote rural area, founded by former freedom fighters and representing a model community for the nation and the world.

Ruheni, Mwangi. *The Minister's Daughter*. Nairobi: Heinemann, 1975.

> Jane Njeri, daughter of a minister from Nyeri, is raised in a strict Christian home. It is the housegirl Grace who introduces Jane to booze and boys, leading to her pregnancy. In this didactic tale, Jane eventually reforms and settles down as a teacher in a rural area near her home.

Ruheni, Mwangi. *The Mystery Smugglers*. Nairobi: Heinemann, 1975. Spear Books.

> Michael Magana becomes involved in an international gang that is trying to corner the world market on uranium.

Ruheni, Mwangi. *The Love Root*. Nairobi: Heinemann, 1976. Spear Books.

> Baby-switching in a Nairobi maternity home and a doctor's problems with impotence are the main events in this novel. Doctor Sam Njogu has to resort to traditional medicine to cure his impotence, but in so doing opens himself to blackmail.

Saisi, Frank (Wilson Kibet arap Sogomo). *The Bhang Syndicate*. Nairobi: Heinemann, 1984. Spear Books.

Paul Kibwalei, a chief inspector with the CID, is assigned to investigate a highly organized and ruthless organization that is responsible for a series of murders in the country. He winds up in the hospital but still manages to smash the racketeering ring.

Tama, Jeremiah. *The Pastor*. Nairobi: Uzima Press, 1978.

Sankaire, a Maasai boy, grows up to become a pastor. Eventually his whole family, including his stubborn father, is baptized.

Waciuma, Charity Wanjiku. *Daughter of Mumbi*. Nairobi: East African Publishing House, 1969.

An autobiographical account of a Kikuyu girl during the Mau Mau conflict, this story includes large sections on traditional customs such as the way names are chosen, polygamy, folktales, and traditional beliefs. Also included are significant sections on the problems arising from the Emergency, especially the way communities were set against each other with the "loyalists" on one side and the "terrorists" on the other, and the results of the Emergency regulations such as curfews and forced labor. We see the political functionaries such as the DCs, chiefs and the local court, and the resistance from independent churches (such as Dini ya Israel or Dini ya Msambwa in Western Kenya led by Elijah Masinde).

Wachira, Godwin. *Ordeal in the Forest*. Nairobi: East African Publishing House, 1968. Modern African Library.

Nundu and his friends have their education interrupted by the outbreak of the Mau Mau Emergency. The story describes their transformation into resistance fighters and the effect of the emergency on the Kikuyu community at large. Important features include the "40 group," the role of vernacular newspapers, oathing, and the armed resistance.

Wambakha, Silvano Onyango Ogessa. *The Way to Power*. Nairobi: East African Literature Bureau, 1974.

On returning to Uganda after studies in the U.S., both Chido and Mwele are given rural administrative postings with the civil service. Mwele changes from an idealistic student to a greedy exploiter of his position and his people. Chido, meanwhile, remains in a rural area without any promotions. At the novel's close, he is faced with a moral dilemma in a dispute between his old friend Mwele and a group of squatters whose houses have been burned down.

Wambakha, Silvano Onyango Ogessa. *The Closed Road to Wapi*. Nairobi: Kenya Literature Bureau, 1978.

Sanyo, a poor peasant from a rural area of a country strikingly like Kenya, makes his way to the capital in search of housing and employment. His uncle, Senator Simba, is a popular politician who espouses socialist ideals but in the end turns out to be an exploitative, urban landlord like many others. The government, the press, the courts, and the rhetoric of socialism are all shown to be ethically bankrupt. In the end, Sanyo hangs himself in despair.

Wambakha, Silvano Onyango Ogessa. *At the Crossroads*. Nairobi: Kenya Literature Bureau, 1982.

When Obaso Omolo graduates from Makerere, he begins a life of self-deception and play-acting. From renaming himself Tabasa—a name that is neither European nor African—to his marriages (he remarries while a student in the U.S.), he creates a series of problems that eventually catch up with him. The novel ends tragically when his wife mistakenly kills their daughter.

Wandai, Karuga. *Mayor in Prison.* Nairobi: East African Educational Publishers, 1993. Spear Books.

Beginning with his childhood in Emergency-era Murang'a, Karuga tells the story of his education, his involvement in politics, and his arrest on charges of misappropriation of funds while serving as the lawyer for a land speculator. After a short but unpleasant stint in Kamiti Prison, Karuga's conviction is overturned by the Kenya Court of Appeal.

Wandera, Billy Ogana. *Hand of Chance.* Nairobi: East African Literature Bureau, 1970. Students' book-writing scheme.

When Ogola goes to the university he has to decide between his high school girlfriend Martha and the new and fascinating Roseline. His family, which is Luo, objects to Roseline because she is Luhya. But love conquers all.

Watene, Kenneth. *Sunset on the Manyatta.* Nairobi: East African Publishing House, 1974.

The coming-of-age story of Nylo "Harry" ole Kantai, a young Maasai from Kenya's Rift Valley region who is the only child of his family to be sent to primary school. Harry excels there and at the secondary school that follows. He eventually travels to Germany for a technical training program and returns to Kenya with a renewed appreciation for his African heritage.

Waweru, Maura. *The Siege*. Nairobi: Kenya Literature Bureau, 1985.

In Ngorongo, a fictional town in Kikuyu country, Wachira and his wife Angelina are the wealthiest couple in the area. When their only daughter is kidnapped and held hostage in a cave, they are traumatized. Kairu, her captor, had been run off the farm where he works because of his attempts to organize the workers. The book is an indictment of neocolonialism and the betrayal of the ideals of independence.

Waweru, P.M. *Judy the Nun*. Nairobi: Longman, 1990. Masterpiece series.

On the eve of independence, Judy Kamati, a rural Kenyan schoolteacher, is given an opportunity to study in the U.S. Her husband vigorously opposes the move, but she goes ahead, positioning herself as a "modern," liberated woman. Although she has plenty of opportunities to be unfaithful to her husband, Judy earns the nickname "the nun" for her chaste behavior. On her return to Kenya, she quickly moves up the career ladder, becoming a dean at her university, an MP, and eventually a cabinet minister—the first woman in Kenya to hold such a post. In the end, however, her husband and an assistant minister kill each other. Repentant, and realizing how "unnatural" her ambitions have been, Judy joins a convent.

Waweru, P.M. *Jackie the Ravenous Pest*. Nairobi: Choro Publishers, 1992.

Young, attractive Jackie Kenda is simultaneously dating Edward Thaka and—following the death of his mother—his wealthy father Patrick. By exploiting her sexuality and her cunning mind, Jackie eventually controls Patrick's life completely, to the point where she runs his life and his business empire. Patrick comes to his senses just in time, however; before he dies, he cuts Jackie out of his will, leaving his wealth to his children. Mainly set in Nairobi, the text focuses on family relations among the new economic elite.

Wegesa, Benjamin S. *Captured by Raiders*. Nairobi: East African Publishing House, 1969.

A juvenile adventure story in which Nanjala, a Bukusu girl, is captured by Tondo (Kalenjin) warriors during a raid in which they kill her father. She lives with the Tondo, taking the new name Chesebe, but escapes when she is ordered to marry the chief. After various adventures, she returns home. An interesting aspect is her grandmother's admonition that Nanjala grow and become a leader for women in a new era when their roles will have changed and when they will have equality with men.

Were, Miriam Khamadi. *The Boy in Between*. Nairobi: Oxford University Press, 1969. Oxford library for East Africa.

Namunyu is "in between" because of his age: too young to join in with his big brothers, but too old play with the little ones. Namunyu is determined to go to school; this is the story of his experience in an elementary school run by a new mission.

Were, Miriam Khamadi. *The Eighth Wife*. Nairobi: East African Publishing House, 1972.

Mulenya, an aging village chief, wants to take the beautiful young Kalimonje as his eighth wife. But she wants to marry his son, Shalimba. Ultimately, Mulenya relents.

Were, Miriam Khamadi. *The High School Gent.* Nairobi: Oxford University Press, 1972.

Namunyu, the hero of Were's earlier novel, *The Boy in Between*, is now in high school and must deal with the usual problems of his age: hazing from bullies, arbitrary discipline, and how to get on with the girls. When Namunyu goes to London for further studies, it is unclear whether his special friendship with Sarah will survive the separation.

Were, Miriam Khamadi. *Your Heart Is My Altar.* Nairobi: East African Publishing House, 1980.

The story of rural interclan rivalries, complicated by religious differences between Muslims, Christians, and followers of traditional African religions. These explode into armed conflict with tragic consequences. The protagonist's father is killed, but she has nonetheless fallen in love with Aluvisia, a Muslim from a rival clan, whose "heart is her altar."

Index